SOCRATES

BY TIM BLAKE NELSON

★

★

DRAMATISTS
PLAY SERVICE
INC.

NOTE ON BILLING

Anyone receiving permission to produce SOCRATES is required to give credit to the Author as sole and exclusive Author of the Play on the title page of all programs distributed in connection with performances of the Play and in all instances in which the title of the Play appears, including printed or digital materials for advertising, publicizing or otherwise exploiting the Play and/or a production thereof. Please see your production license for font size and typeface requirements.

Be advised that there may be additional credits required in all programs and promotional material. Such language will be listed under the "Additional Billing" section of production licenses. It is the licensee's responsibility to ensure any and all required billing is included in the requisite places, per the terms of the license.

SPECIAL NOTE ON SONGS/RECORDINGS

Dramatists Play Service neither holds the rights to nor grants permission to use any songs or recordings mentioned in the Play. Permission for performances of copyrighted songs, arrangements or recordings mentioned in this Play is not included in our license agreement. The permission of the copyright owner(s) must be obtained for any such use. For any songs and/or recordings mentioned in the Play, other songs, arrangements, or recordings may be substituted provided permission from the copyright owner(s) of such songs, arrangements or recordings is obtained; or songs, arrangements or recordings in the public domain may be substituted.

For my mother, Ruth Nelson
B.A. Philosophy '58, Bryn Mawr College

The world premiere of SOCRATES was presented by the Public Theater (Oskar Eustis, Artistic Director; Patrick Willingham, Executive Director), opening in April 2019. It was directed by Doug Hughes, the set design was by Scott Pask, the costume design was by Catherine Zuber, the lighting design was by Tyler Micoleau, the sound design and original music were by Mark Bennett, and the production stage manager was Theresa Flanagan. The cast was as follows:

SOCRATES	Michael Stuhlbarg
PLATO	Teagle F. Bougere
A BOY	Niall Cunningham
PROXENUS/ARISTOPHANES/GORGIAS	Tom Nelis
XANTHIPPE	Miriam A. Hyman
THE ARCHON/MEGASTHENES	Lee Wilkof
ALCIBIADES/SIMMIAS	Austin Smith
AGATHON/MENO	Joe Tapper
ERYXIMACHUS/ANYTUS/GUARD	David Aaron Baker
CRITO/CHAEREPHON/MELETUS THE ELDER	Robert Joy
AENESIDEMOS/LAMPROCLES	Karl Green
DIOKLES/MELETUS	Dave Quay
LYCON/THRASYMACHUS/POLUS	Peter Jay Fernandez
ANDROMACHUS/AETIOS	Alan Mendez
ENSEMBLE	Daniel Reece, Ro Boddie

SOCRATES was developed with the support of New York Stage and Film & Vassar's Powerhouse Season, Summer 2016.

CHARACTERS

SOCRATES

PLATO

A BOY

PROXENUS

XANTHIPPE

THE ARCHON

Followers of Socrates

ALCIBIADES

AGATHON

ARISTOPHANES

ERYXIMACHUS

CRITO

APOLLODORUS

ARISTEDEMUS

PAUSANIUS

CHAEREPHON

AENESIDEMOS

ANTISTHENES

SIMMIAS

Followers of Socrates and Eventual Tyrants

DIOKLES

THERAMENES

CRITIAS

The Accusers

ANYTUS

LYCON

MELETUS

The Interlocutors

MENO

THRASYMACHUS

POLYMEDES

MELETUS THE ELDER

MEGASTHENES

GORGIAS

CALLICLES

POLUS

Others

ANDROMACHUS

ANDROCLES

LAMPROCLES

SOPHRONISCUS

AETIOS

POISONER

GUARD

VARIOUS COUNCIL AND CROWD MEMBERS

SERVANTS AND REVELERS

NOTE

The play should be performed fluidly, boisterously, and with pace. A theatrical inventiveness is essential, as is a driving passion for the ideas and arguments. Though a play of many words, it is not to be performed as a series of inert conversations, but rather as mental struggle assayed eagerly, often with humor and sometimes rage. The stakes could not be higher, leading eventually to a great thinker's life being held in the balance.

Theaters are encouraged to cast as many or as few actors as works for the production. Gender- and racially diverse casting is also encouraged.

SOCRATES

ACT ONE

Lights reveal a Boy, fifteen. Plato and Proxenus stand apart.

PROXENUS. It's certainly not how I expected it.

PLATO. Athens?

PROXENUS. Athens. Yes.

PLATO. We've been through a great deal.

PROXENUS. There's an unease in your city.

PLATO. You're not wrong.

PROXENUS. But we're extremely grateful.

PLATO. As am I, if the boy's reputation is to be believed.

PROXENUS. I'll let you be the judge. His father was a remarkable man.

PLATO. So I've been told.

PROXENUS. He would have wanted me to bring the boy here. To you. He has some ideas he's written down…

PLATO. I'm eager to read them.

 Pause.

Was there something else?

PROXENUS. No. It's just—

PLATO. Please.

PROXENUS. His father was a physician. Physician to the king. I know you don't have that sort of thing here.

 Pause.

A king.

PLATO. I'm familiar with the concept, and certainly appreciate its efficiencies.

PROXENUS. The boy loved his father. Followed him everywhere. A man of science and facts.

PLATO. Yes.

PROXENUS. He gave the boy things I simply can't, which is partly why I've brought him to you. It's been...

PLATO. I can imagine.

PROXENUS. Like his father, he can be unforgiving. Relentless.

PLATO. I'll manage.

> *Pause.*

PROXENUS. I'm sure you will.

> *Proxenus leaves.*

PLATO. Well then. Here we are.

> *Silence.*

Have you been here before?

> *No response.*

Have you been to Athens before?

> *Pause.*

How are you finding it? The city?

BOY. I find it murderous.

PLATO. Murderous?

BOY. In every face. A city that killed its greatest thinker. Killed him like a traitor. Why did they do that?

PLATO. This is not a topic I wish to discuss.

BOY. Because you're not capable? It's somehow too daunting for the great Plato?

PLATO. No.

BOY. Because you're an Athenian?

PLATO. What's that supposed to mean?

BOY. You're an Athenian. The Athenians killed him. My question therefore implicates you, especially in the context of a democracy where leaders and their actions are promulgated as representing the people's will.

    A pause.

PLATO. This is not beginning well.

BOY. In Macedonia they reported it to have been inevitable. I find that troubling.

PLATO. Troubling?

BOY. Meaning there was no other option.

PLATO. I know the meaning of the word inevitable.

BOY. So? He had to die? Did he?

    Plato does not respond.

It's a simple question.

PLATO. You know nothing of democracy. You couldn't possibly, not having lived in one. And it's not a simple question.

BOY. Why?

PLATO. Because nothing about him was simple. He was in fact utterly confounding.

BOY. How?

PLATO. We're not—No.

BOY. Please.

    A long pause.

PLATO. He was both ugly and beautiful, crass and eloquent, unkempt and impeccable. Unspeakably, arrogantly rude, and we all loved him desperately. Will that suffice?

BOY. It doesn't answer the question.

PLATO. He had every opportunity not to die. Time and again we begged him. You can't imagine the heartbreak.

BOY. Then?

PLATO. This isn't the purpose of—

BOY. Why would I come here…to study with you—

PLATO. That has yet to be agreed on. If your guardian didn't explain, I'm evaluating you.

BOY. Evaluate all you want. Why would I listen to any of what you have to say without knowing why you even remain in a city that—

PLATO. Enough.

BOY. That would kill the man to whom you've devoted your life? A city that supposedly allows people to speak as they choose. And couldn't they do the same to you? To me?

PLATO. I don't yet know you, and I'm not him.

BOY. You've spent your life writing his words.

PLATO. Have I?

BOY. Almost every dialogue is filled with what he said.

PLATO. Most of them aren't actually.

BOY. That's a lie.

PLATO. I assure you it's not.

BOY. In every single one—

PLATO. He's the main character, yes.

BOY. So you can't spend a few minutes…

PLATO. It would be a lot more than a few minutes.

BOY. …speaking about your own teacher?

PLATO. He wasn't my teacher.

BOY. Another lie.

PLATO. Enough with that. The fact is he would despise me for the very relationship you and I now seem to be negotiating. You were going to show me—Your guardian said you'd written some—

BOY. Why would he have been against your teaching me?

PLATO. My teaching anyone. Anyone teaching anyone.

BOY. Now I have to know.

PLATO. And I'm telling you—

    The Boy rises.

Where are you going?

BOY. I'll learn more walking the city. I could speak with any stranger and get more than these mumbling prevarications.

12

PLATO. "Prevarications"?

And the Boy is gone.

Wait.

He returns.

I've determined there might be some use in it.

BOY. You've determined?

PLATO. Some terms though. Ones that I set, and not you.

BOY. May I hear them?

PLATO. That when we're done, we work.

BOY. What else would we do?

PLATO. And that you truly listen. To understand, really to understand, this can't just be about him, because you were right: As with any society that supposes leaders reflect its will, it'll involve the city where you hope to study. A city that's still recovering, as your guardian was wise enough to observe, from years of turmoil: plague, war, even tyranny.

BOY. Tyranny?

PLATO. So few understand what it was really like—and certainly not you with your needling presumptions. Even those who lived through it still grapple with whether our system has any of its self-proclaimed efficacy at all. Democracy when it was new and messy and fragile, filled with nervous wrath.

A pause.

And I loved him beyond what I could possibly describe which, if you must know, is why it's difficult for me even to dare try. And I speak as the one who betrayed him in perhaps the worst way possible.

BOY. You betrayed him?

PLATO. In a sense I betrayed him more profoundly and lastingly than Athens did.

BOY. How?

PLATO. In time. In time. But above all, you must have patience, for in spite of how you're coming off right now, there is much you don't know.

BOY. It's possible.

PLATO. In fact, by the time we're done, you might determine you know nothing at all. I'll start not with how I saw him, but how others did. And one man in particular, who loved him in his way more than anyone.

Lights reveal Alcibiades.

I first encountered this man myself when I wasn't much older than you. He was a general at the time, and the city's darling: charismatic, brilliant, beautiful, and of regal stock—the nephew of Pericles in fact, and at the pinnacle of his career, about to lead the navy in our expansion west. The very physical and mental embodiment of all Athens stood for.

Plato guides the Boy to a chair at the edge of a raucous scene lit by candles.

ALCIBIADES. Why should I bother with Plato? He's not going to say a word!

PLATO. *(To the Boy.)* You'll smile when he addresses you, because of course he's right. In those early years I hardly speak.

This gathering of unashamedly drunk Greek men includes the playwright Aristophanes, a doctor named Eryximachus, Aristedemus, Pausanius, their host the poet Agathon, and a dignified man named Crito. Plato to the Boy:

Smile!

The Boy (as young Plato) does.

BOY. I'm smiling.

PLATO. Perfect.

Alcibiades tousles the Boy's hair.

ALCIBIADES. You see, not a peep from the boy!

PLATO. It's a world more full of wit, passion, and above all ideas than anything you ever imagined possible. In fact, you know from this moment on it will be your life.

ALCIBIADES. More wine!

PLATO. His name was Alcibiades, and he had the room in his thrall, but the focus, as ever, was Socrates.

Lights reveal Socrates, in his mid-fifties.

ALCIBIADES. Fill everyone's cup who hasn't got any, but particularly his. Not that it'll make any difference. It pours right down into his gut to replenish the lagoon there, having no effect.

ERYXIMACHUS. You think we're a bunch of savages, Alcibiades? Drinking without a prayer?

ALCIBIADES. Listen to this!

AGATHON. Before you came in we were giving speeches about Love.

ALCIBIADES. Socrates?

AGATHON. Him too.

ALCIBIADES. And you believed a single word?

CRITO. His was beautiful.

ALCIBIADES. Of course you'd say that, Crito. But then he interrupted everyone else's with questions.

CRITO. Never.

ALCIBIADES. Explained how each of you is wrong, but that he knows nothing and is totally ignorant about everything, making you wonder how he can have his unwelcome opinion in the first place?!

SOCRATES. I spoke my speech and that was it.

ALCIBIADES. Well I can tell you this: As soon as I utter a syllable about anything, he'll be strangling me for not talking about him.

SOCRATES. Nonsense!

ERYXIMACHUS. Here's an idea: *(To Alcibiades.)* Why don't you give a speech about Socrates?

CRITO. Now that would make my evening.

All shout in agreement.

ALCIBIADES. Shall I?

SOCRATES. Not if you're going to make me out like an idiot.

ARISTOPHANES. ESPECIALLY if you're going to make him out like an idiot!

ALCIBIADES. If I speak I'll tell the truth; give you the whole man.

SOCRATES. You have to or I WILL strangle you.

15

ALCIBIADES. Already you can see he's getting nervous…spittling and foaming…

Socrates wipes his mouth.

I'm going to begin in all seriousness by comparing him to one of those sileni you see on the doorposts of the temple of Dionysos. You've all seen them, grinning like demons, the mouth wide and hideous, a flute in their hands, but if you split them down the middle, they've got the Gods inside. Of course whereas the sileni bewitch listeners with melodies, Socrates does it with words—not unctions or medicines like Eryximachus or poetry like Agathon, or plays like Aristophanes—

ARISTOPHANES. Thank you.

ALCIBIADES. But with questions and arguments, until all of Athens is under his spell.

CRITO. Or all of Athens despises him.

Alcibiades turns to Socrates.

ALCIBIADES. When I hear you speak I retreat into a quiet kind of rage, my heart pushing at my teeth.

The men nod in assent, the mood growing bemusedly serious.

I've heard my own uncle hold forth, and every general and statesman you can name. I fancy myself an orator. You have to be to get anywhere in this greatest city on earth, the envy of all of Greece. *(Pointing to Socrates.)* But no one turns my soul inside out like he does. He makes me feel like I can't go on living like I do, and you can't deny it, Socrates.

SOCRATES. Am I allowed to answer?

EVERYONE. No!

SOCRATES. Because if this is going to be one of your endless disquisitions—

ALCIBIADES. That's exactly what it's going to be.

SOCRATES. I beg of you. I'd prefer lighting myself ablaze!

ALCIBIADES. He convinces me that any time I spend on politics I'm neglecting what's truly important. And since politics are my life, my very life is a sham. So what's left but to avoid him, stay away? And yet for the life of me I can't. To tell the truth, I wish he were dead, but if he were, I'd be so racked with grief I couldn't go on living. Just look at him there, scowling like a corpulent Medusa. Why is everyone laughing? There's nothing funny about him. He's a scourge! A curse! The worst thing that ever happened to this city! But enough praise. Because I'll tell you another way he's like a satyr. How he's obsessed with good-looking boys—

SOCRATES. No!

ALCIBIADES. And the less clothing the better. He can't tear his eyes from them.

SOCRATES. No sir!

ALCIBIADES. Somehow he finds himself at the gymnasium daily, claiming the need for shade, or to exercise himself, though he'll sit there on the bench not moving a flaccid muscle, bending the ear of any cherubic buck who'll come near about temperance and virtue, all the while sneaking glances at the hotspot lest there be any movement there!

> *The men roar.*

SOCRATES. Not a word of it true! Look here!

> *He flexes a muscle that's anything but flaccid.*

ALCIBIADES. Not true he says! At the gymnasium daily, but a belly the size of a stove!

> *Laughter.*

Not…not that he'll ever do anything about it. Try and make sense of that. Lurking around the gymnasium and baths, leering like a pervert fit for exile, and won't so much as touch the bodies of the boys he clearly covets!

SOCRATES. I've truly had enough.

ALCIBIADES. And I'll prove it, because I used to catch him ogling me.

SOCRATES. Never!

ALCIBIADES. Oh yes! And I wasn't upset about it either. Just yield up a few succulent favors, I figured, and get all the wisdom he had to offer.

SOCRATES. You said you'd tell the truth!

ALCIBIADES. Every word!

SOCRATES. Every word as you choose to remember it!

ARISTOPHANES. Quiet, Socrates!

CRITO. Go on, Alcibiades.

ALCIBIADES. I was clever and deliberate, and when I went to meet him I left my slave at home so the two of us could be alone, expecting of course to hear lovers' whispers, sweet nothings in praise of my beauty, the tenor of my voice, the shape of my leg. But other than a lot of speeches and endless infuriating questions—

SOCRATES. Yes!

ALCIBIADES. Not a word but goodbye.

SOCRATES. Fine! Exactly!

ALCIBIADES. Well, I said to myself, this won't do. I convinced him to go to the gymnasium, and even made sure we had the place to ourselves. We stretched and lifted. And of course we wrestled. Time and time again—I made sure of that—until completely exhausted, the both of us. And nothing. Except bruises on my arms and back that would last for days.

SOCRATES. So much for my flaccid muscles!

ALCIBIADES. I've never been so sore, but in all the wrong places! Yet as you all know, I'm not one to be deterred. I invited him to dinner, making myself the seducer. The first time, I couldn't get him to stay past the meal. The final bite and he was off like a relay runner. But I persevered, inviting him again, this time attenuating the visit, adding more food and drink, but most of all talk, his favorite nourishment, late into the night. How better to keep him there than to let him ask me questions, of which as usual he had many.

SOCRATES. Yes.

ALCIBIADES. Go ahead. Tell them.

SOCRATES. Tell them what?

ALCIBIADES. The questions.

SOCRATES. That second dinner? What is friendship? What is love? Is there purpose to hate? was an especially incisive one. We spent a good two hours parsing the word's etymology and usage, going back to the Mycenaeans.

ALCIBIADES. You can imagine my keen interest. I sought penetration of an entirely different order. Again, he rose to leave. "You can't walk home now," I said. To which he responded:

SOCRATES. This was fifteen years ago.

ALCIBIADES. Then we'll have to make due with my version after all.

SOCRATES. "A walk will do me good, Alcibiades." Something like that.

ALCIBIADES. To which I said: "In two hours it'll be light. Then you can go home." I called servants. Had them clear two tables and bring blankets. Socrates was confused.

SOCRATES. Not as confused as you think.

ALCIBIADES. "This way we can keep talking while we drift off."

SOCRATES. I asked about your parents, what they would think about our "drifting off" together, my not having sought permission for what didn't interest me in the first place.

ALCIBIADES. And I answered, "What about them?" For I had been bitten, and not by a snake but something far more venomous. And looking around—at Agathon, Aristophanes, Eryximachus, Crito... we're all paralyzed by this sweet and awful poison, this sacred spiritual rage. Even Socrates, though he's the one doing the biting. Of course, the snake doesn't suffer from the poison of his own venom.

SOCRATES. The way I remember it, I went to sleep.

ALCIBIADES. Once he'd laid down, I began a quiet, relentless assault. "Socrates?"

SOCRATES. What?

ALCIBIADES. No—what happened between us—you must play yourself.

SOCRATES. This is becoming insufferable. I'd sooner have capitulated to your night of debauchery than have to participate in this unmitigated ludicrousness any longer.

ALCIBIADES. Shall I continue then?

SOCRATES. I don't care what you do.

ALCIBIADES. You're certain. We shall have my version?

SOCRATES. Did I not say?

ALCIBIADES. He instructed me in the gentlest of terms to lie supine, clutch the backs of my knees and expose my backhatch for the taking.

The room roars.

SOCRATES. HE LIES!

ALCIBIADES. What's your version then?

SOCRATES. As I said, I went to sleep. I went to sleep. Not facing you I might add, to make my intentions, or lack thereof, perfectly clear!

ALCIBIADES. Shall we play it out then? Now will you deign to participate?

SOCRATES. Fine.

ALCIBIADES. "Socrates," I said.

SOCRATES. "Yes?"

ALCIBIADES. "You're awake?"

SOCRATES. "It would appear."

ALCIBIADES. "Face me."

SOCRATES. Which I then did.

ALCIBIADES. "You want to know something?"

SOCRATES. "What is it, Alcibiades?"

ALCIBIADES. "You're the only lover I've ever had who's worthy of me."

SOCRATES. "Lover?"

ALCIBIADES. "It's clear what we both want. There's no man with more to offer me, and if that means I repay you with what I can give, it's worth it to be transformed by your wisdom."

SOCRATES. Now suddenly we tread the fields of accuracy. Exactly what you said.

ALCIBIADES. And what was your extremely arrogant response?

SOCRATES. "Alcibiades, I have no doubt you will one day lead Athens…on the field of battle or in the Assembly. Both, likely."

ALCIBIADES. You predicted well.

SOCRATES. "But the kind of beauty I have, if traded for yours, would be like my parting with gold after you've given me tin," is what I said.

ALCIBIADES. Exactly. "Few would agree with you," I countered. Which of course was the stupidest thing I could have said. What was his response? Anyone!

CRITO. He asked if you expected him to think as others do.

SOCRATES. Thank you Crito. Yes. Exactly what Crito said I said.

ALCIBIADES. To which I responded: "Perhaps this once, think as others do." And you answered?

SOCRATES. "Then say you're right. Is it your contention, Alcibiades, that what I have to give is for sale, and what's more, for bodily pleasure?"

ALCIBIADES. "I've tendered my offer."

SOCRATES. I then promised to think it over and determine what was best, studying it from every side, as with any topic that would interest us.

ALCIBIADES. "Any topic that would interest us." That's what he made of my entreaties.

SOCRATES. Unlike with you, sir, bodily pleasures do not subordinate all others.

ALCIBIADES. Yet somehow I was certain my arrow had hit its mark. Without a word, I stripped naked—a teenager mind you, like Plato here, but forgive me, with a face and physique as unrivaled as they are now. A flower for the plucking.

SOCRATES. Must we listen to this?

EVERYONE. Yes!

SOCRATES. He goes on and on...! *(Pointing at Aristophanes.)* It's worse than his last two plays!

ALCIBIADES. I put my garment over him, and climbed into his bed, holding him in my arms.

SOCRATES. Then what happened?

ALCIBIADES. I caressed, I fondled, but by the end of that night I'd no more "slept" with him than if I'd shared a bed with a father or brother.

SOCRATES. Exactly.

ALCIBIADES. But his rejection only made me more subservient. I followed him everywhere, devouring every word. Day after day, from the Agora to the law courts, the port to the gymnasium, as he questioned anyone, no matter how stupid or unwashed.

SOCRATES. I'll hear none of that.

ALCIBIADES. It's true! Here you are among us, the city's brightest and most worthy, but in the morning while we're all sleeping it off you'll be at the docks or the market learning how to bone and gut a fish or slice a turnip from some toothless indigent as if you're in the presence of Hesiod or Homer. You're the only true democrat I'll call a friend.

CRITO. What about the rest of us?

ALCIBIADES. You're certainly my friends…

SOCRATES. Have you any idea the trouble your admiration has caused me?

ALCIBIADES. Never lovers, but everyone thinks we were! If anything it's been to your advantage!

SOCRATES. Not the sort of advantage I'm after.

ALCIBIADES. To be considered my mentor? Athens adores me, I adore you, therefore Athens adores you. The perfect syllogism. And who encourages me to think that way?

EVERYONE. Socrates! He does!

ALCIBIADES. You've taught an entire generation how to think!

SOCRATES. That's simply not true!

ALCIBIADES. "Not true." Not long after, we were both called into service at Potidaea, and I tell you he endured the hardships of war better than anyone.

SOCRATES. What hardships?

CRITO. Is that a joke?

ALCIBIADES. Crito was there. The rest of us donned sheepskins and felt, whatever could shield us from head to toe, but Socrates?

CRITO. The same filthy coat he wore in Athens.

ALCIBIADES. And complained less about trudging the ice on his bare feet than we did in our wrappings and shoes.

SOCRATES. With my toes I could clutch at the ice.

ALCIBIADES. When you couldn't feel your toes?

SOCRATES. Did you ever see me slip?

ALCIBIADES. Our supplies were cut off, and he never joined the rest of us to grouse about the rationing.

SOCRATES. It wouldn't have made food appear.

ALCIBIADES. Perhaps complaining distracted us from fearing death.

SOCRATES. Another folly.

ALCIBIADES. Fearing death is a folly?

CRITO. This he told me when walking daily throughout the city at the height of the plague.

ALCIBIADES. I'm too drunk to argue that one. Which brings to mind the question, has anyone here ever seen Socrates drunk?

EVERYONE. No. Of course not! Never!

SOCRATES. I drink to live, not the other way around like the rest of you.

ARISTOPHANES. Yes we've all heard that one before. And you eat to live, you don't live to eat. Your present girth suggests otherwise!

Laughter.

SOCRATES. Hilarious. Truly hilarious, Aristophanes. Perhaps you should have put that in your so-called comedy of which I was inexplicably the focus. Why do I squander my time on any of you?

ALCIBIADES. You can't help it! You love us!

ARISTOPHANES. The subject of our evening!

Applause.

SOCRATES. I see.

ALCIBIADES. We were at Potidaea through the summer. One morning, as we went about organizing camp at dawn, there stood Socrates in the middle of it all, oblivious, lost in thought. By lunch he was still there, hadn't moved a toe, endeavoring, it would seem, to puzzle out some question that had vexed him since sunrise. By this time we all began to notice, wondering how long it would go on. Some of the Ionians and I laid our beds outside, just to see if he'd stand there all night. Which of course he did. I woke time and time again, and still he was there. He never uttered a word, nor did we ask, but at dawn he addressed the Gods and went about his day, the wiser for it to be sure, but how, or with what new understanding, to this moment I couldn't tell you. What did you discover?

SOCRATES. You wish me to share some truth I learned?

ALCIBIADES. Something like that.

SOCRATES. In such moments I am not learning but unlearning, so I'm afraid I cannot help you.

ALCIBIADES. I should say so. Why would I need to unlearn?

SOCRATES. In your case sir, having only our present lifespans, there's insufficient time to list the reasons.

AGATHON. How was he as a soldier?

SOCRATES. I did what was expected of me.

ALCIBIADES. Ha!

AGATHON. Tell us, Alcibiades.

ALCIBIADES. The fighting was brutal on the peninsula. I performed bravely to be sure. We all did. But no one more than Socrates. I'd been thrown from my horse and was surrounded by hoplites. He bound me up and stayed with me there, fending off attackers, then carried me over a field of the dead back to our camp. Perdiccas himself offered decorations. Socrates refused. He's never once mentioned saving my life.

SOCRATES. By saving you I was saving myself.

ALCIBIADES. I remember him best finally at Delium.

SOCRATES. An end in sight!

ALCIBIADES. We had surrounded a contingent from Thespiae, but in doing so had wheeled back, and not knowing who was who, began to slaughter many of our own. After Delium we wore uniforms. But there Athenian killed Athenian. Socrates again served in the line, and when we'd at last organized a retreat, the Boeotians met us head on, and I beheld him there. He might as well have been strutting through Athens, as proud and oblivious as a pelican, his sword brandished, ready to take on all comers. And in this way I will always see him: a most unlikely deity among men. Fearless and clearheaded on a battlefield where soldiers mindlessly kill even their own. Never bending, never yielding, always conspicuously and unashamedly who and what he is: a man, thinker, spirit, and, most of all, friend such as neither Athens nor the world has ever known.

Pause.

And so concludes my eulogy.

SOCRATES. Thank the Gods.

ALCIBIADES. Even after that he ridicules me!

Theramenes and Critias burst in, led by Diokles.

DIOKLES. Alcibiades?! Where is he?! With Socrates! Of course!

SOCRATES. Diokles? And who's that? Theramenes? Critias?

CRITO. What would a gathering be without our overprivileged youth?!

DIOKLES. Overprivileged youth? We are simply the worshippers of Socrates.

SOCRATES. That I can't help.

CRITO. That they're overprivileged, or worship you?

DIOKLES. Wine!

CRITO. Is there enough? What says our host? Agathon?

AGATHON. Pour! Pour!

ARISTOPHANES. Let's leave some for the rest of us.

DIOKLES. Worry not. We've plans elsewhere, hither and yon!

A cup is passed over and enjoyed. Diokles looks to Alcibiades.

So?

ALCIBIADES. It's time! *(To the room.)* Now I'll depart, and leave you filthy old bastards to speechify. You make your statements, and we'll make ours!

CRITO. What's that supposed to mean?

ALCIBIADES. Where's my slave? Andromachus!

Andromachus, slave to Alcibiades, appears.

Why empty-handed?

ANDROMACHUS. I've been waiting in the courtyard.

ALCIBIADES. Fetch what we brought, imbecile.

SOCRATES. Why not stay? All of you. Agathon?

AGATHON. Of course!

ALCIBIADES. Don't I wish we could!

CRITO. Something tells me you're not off to rehearse battle plans.

ALCIBIADES. Sicily, sir, will soon kneel under the Athenian boot, but no, we've concerns of another sort this evening!

CRITO. I see.

ALCIBIADES. But let it be known: Everything about me... *(Points flamboyantly to Socrates.)* I owe to him!

> *Applause.*
> *The street.*
> *Alcibiades and the revelers huddle.*

All right then.

> *Andromachus holds five poles hewn from tree branches. Alcibiades passes them around, keeping one for himself. Earthen statues depicting a naked Hermes appear suspended: big square heads and erect phalluses protrude skyward at an angle.*

Let's see what our devout citizens and their mighty Gods make of this!

> *Alcibiades scampers below the one nearest, winds up with his pole, and smacks the statue hard. It tumbles to the ground, breaking into pieces.*
>
> *Alcibiades runs to the next and does the same. The revelers follow, smashing every "Herm" they see.*

BOY. What were they?

PLATO. Herms. Little statues of Hermes. Hundreds of them above doorposts all over Athens, and they smashed every one in the city.

BOY. Why?

PLATO. An act of aristocratic derision, plain and simple. "Elitist," it was called, which it was. A thumb in the eye of the common people. And though he had no part of it, for Socrates, the smashing of the Herms by his most famous pupil was the beginning of what would be the case against him.

> *Dawn.*
> *Citizens appear, see the carnage of sacred stone.*

26

BOY. The smashing of little statues? Truthfully?

PLATO. Manifestations of a God. Don't underestimate the stupidity of Athenians.

> *Anytus, fifties, picks up the head of a Herm as a citizen wheels in a tumbril already filled. Citizens clear the floor, adding to the heaped vessel.*

We were at war. On the eve of the great campaign to Sicily, blood-thirsty gamble that it was, and to be led by Alcibiades himself. Would anyone now come back alive?

> *Anytus, with a man named Androcles, comes forward, the loaded barrow beside him. He speaks as though to many.*

ANYTUS. The blood of every Athenian soldier who perishes in Sicily shall be on the hands of those who have done this! We will find who was responsible, and subject them to the severest penalties our laws allow. For I tell you, this is worse than the worst crime against man! This attacks the Gods who keep us safe and free.

ANDROCLES. As our good friend Anytus suggests, if it attacks our Gods, it attacks our democracy! When war threatens us all!

PLATO. Hundreds of soldiers were loosed on the city. No one had seen anything like it. Husbands, sons, fathers were all taken in. Anyone who'd ever lifted a cup in a club or spoken a word against the Gods was seized. And, just as importantly, their slaves.

> *Andromachus, beaten and bloodied, soldiers at each elbow, is shoved down onto a stool before Androcles and Anytus.*

ANYTUS. Alcibiades led the entire group. True?

> *Andromachus doesn't answer.*

Are you aware of the consequences to a slave for withholding information from the people of Athens?

> *No response.*

ANDROCLES. Or that providing information could gain you freedom?

ANDROMACHUS. I have parents, a young wife. Freedom for them as well?

ANYTUS. What do you know?

ANDROMACHUS. A blasphemy far worse than smashing statues.

ANYTUS. How could that be?

ANDROMACHUS. Far worse.

> *The house of Alcibiades.*
> *The room lit by candles, Alcibiades, dressed as the goddess Persephone, stands with Diokles, dressed as Hades.*
> *Behind them a slave mixes a brew.*
> *Initiates crouch on all fours, while members of Alcibiades' drinking club hover over them.*
> *The slave hands Alcibiades a cup, from which Alcibiades drinks.*

ALCIBIADES. I have fasted. I have drunk the kykeon. I have taken from the kiste!

> *He passes the cup to Diokles, who drinks and passes it on to the other members, who do the same.*

We now expose things done, things shown, and things said! For I am Persephone, daughter to Zeus and Demeter!

DIOKLES. And I am great Hades! Deliver the punishment, earthly priests!

> *The initiates are flogged with enormous corn stalks.*

ALCIBIADES. Sit up, foul initiates, and take from the cup!

> *The initiates rise to kneeling positions. Diokles passes down a second cup.*

And behold how great Hades defiles his concubine Persephone as winter rages on the neglected earth!

> *Crazed music. Diokles as Hades mounts Alcibiades as Persephone and simulates a violent, rapacious sodomy: a psychedelic carnival of sexual abandon.*
> *The Boy and Plato.*

PLATO. They profaned the Eleusinian Mysteries.

BOY. The what?

PLATO. The Eleusinian Mysteries. Religious rites sacred to the cult of Demeter. A sacrilege beyond imagining in a city mad about its Gods. They might as well have destroyed the Parthenon for all the hysteria that followed. By the time it was revealed, Alcibiades had left for Sicily, where the Spartans killed fifty thousand of our men. Fifty thousand slaughtered. They sank our entire fleet. Every ship. All blamed on lampooning our divine protectors. But something far more dangerous lay behind this sacrilege. Hatred for the democracy, its customs and all they stood for.

BOY. Did Socrates hate the democracy?

PLATO. He questioned it.

BOY. Do you?

PLATO. Excuse me?

BOY. Do you.

PLATO. Who wants to know?

BOY. The person asking.

>*A long silence.*

PLATO. We're not talking about me.

BOY. No?

PLATO. Not on that topic.

>*A pause.*

Alcibiades was sentenced to death. Murdered in the end as a fugitive in Phrygia.

BOY. And Socrates?

PLATO. He too of course would stand trial—though it took years to bring the charges—and in front of all Athens.

>*Socrates, now seventy, his beard and hair longer and more scraggly, his eyes as fierce as ever, stands barefoot, his clothes and skin filthy.*

Did your father ever tell you about our trials here?

BOY. My guardian says they're unfair.

PLATO. Why does he say that?

BOY. He says the dikastai aren't equipped to judge.

PLATO. The dikastai of whom he speaks number five hundred and one, drawn by lot from those citizens who register. A simple majority prevails. Guilty or not. A process, shall we say, aggressively devoid of nuance.

Lights reveal the Archon.

In judgment stands the Archon, who has allowed the complaint to go forward. Socrates had three accusers instead of the customary one. They represented the pillars of society that resented him most.

Lights reveal the accusers as they are named and described:

Meletus for the poets—his father and grandfather poets before him, Lycon for the politicians.

Anytus stands center.

And finally, Anytus, for the trades.

Anytus addresses the dikastai—in this case the theater audience.

ANYTUS. I am a simple tanner of hides. I'm not here for a personal vendetta. Many times have I interacted with the accused, usually on the most friendly of terms. I'm not here for Meletus nor Lycon, nor myself, nor for any individual, but for Athens. Isn't that why each of us has gathered here? For decades Socrates and his followers have desecrated our government and our Gods, ridiculing both with an arrogance that has delivered ruin. We will not forget the smashing of the Herms. We will not forget the profanation of the Mysteries. For Socrates and those he teaches, it's as if there's not one Athens but two: one for them, and one for the rest of us. We lost a war. We lost a way of life we're desperate to rebuild. Think of this great experiment we have dared and all that each of you has risked and sacrificed in its service. Take just a moment to consider this city and the unprecedented system of government, by the people and answerable to the people, it dares to advance. Think of the disdain felt toward you, the people, by the corrupt elite who resent the power democracy vests in you, with their private drinking parties and secret societies and the plague of vile desecration they spread. Think of their shameless contempt for the founding ideas of Solon, of Cleisthenes, of Pericles, who took power from themselves and gave it to you. And so in summation we say this: If you abominate the idea that the people should rule, and you prefer the tyranny of the wealthy and so-called educated few, you are not welcome here. If you would worship Gods other than those who protect us, you are not welcome here. If you would corrupt our youth, and have the son turn on the father in vicious assault against all that is sacred and true, you are not welcome. If you would question democracy in the very place of its birth, and go so far as to attack repeatedly in the public square the laws and truths we hold dear, and the leaders who defend them, Athens will not have you. We have come too far and lost too much to have some live by their own rules and others not. Socrates has weakened this state, he has corrupted its youth, he has attacked relentlessly its institutions. For the good of Athens and all she represents, for these specific charges: He has worshiped Gods not sanctioned by Athens, he has practiced atheism, and he has corrupted the youth of Athens, finally we say, Socrates must die.

> *Anytus steps back. The Archon rises.*

ARCHON. Should he choose, Socrates will now answer his accusers.

> *The Archon sits as Socrates steps forward.*

SOCRATES. I can't say what effect these three have had on you, but they've almost persuaded me. It was especially galling earlier when Anytus cautioned you to beware my gifts as a speaker. I have no such gifts, unless a great orator is one who strives to pursue only truth. I'll respond therefore not with the flowery prolixity or the angry bluster to which you've become accustomed in arenas such as this, but in the language of the open spaces of our city where a good many of you have encountered me. How do I vex Athenian democracy and all it holds dear? With what dangerous ideas do I concern myself and our youth, thereby corrupting them and challenging sanctioned Gods? What I do is simple: I speak with those who will speak, and I question those who will answer, allowing them in turn to question me.

> *The Agora.*
> *Socrates, grimy, barefoot and disheveled and in his element, engages with a raucous group of men that includes Meno, Crito, and others. The energy is aggressive, fervent, immediate, and loud.*

MENO. So I'm to tell everyone that Socrates has no idea what virtue is?!

SOCRATES. You can say that, and that Socrates has never met anyone who does!

> *A shout from the crowd. Plato leads the Boy to seat him right*

at Socrates's feet.

PLATO. You are right next to him, so you don't miss a syllable.

SOCRATES. Young Plato here will tell you. *(To the Boy.)* Have I ever claimed even to have met someone who can tell me what virtue is?

BOY. Has he?

PLATO. Of course not.

BOY. You haven't.

SOCRATES. And he's here every single day!

Meno shouts over the ensuing din.

MENO. You didn't meet Gorgias when he was here?!

SOCRATES. Perhaps I did, but I'm a forgetful and absent-minded old man...

The audience laughs, ready for the fight to come.

MENO. No, no, Socrates. I'm not falling for this nonsense.

SOCRATES. Nonsense he says, and I admit I don't know a thing about anything!

MENO. All lies!

SOCRATES. Leave Gorgias out of it since he's not here, the lucky blowhard, and tell me what YOU think virtue is.

MENO. Shall I?

The assembled crowd cheers its assent.

MAN. Tell him!

ANOTHER MAN. Get on with it!

MENO. Easy! If it's manly virtue, it involves running the city's affairs so that one helps friends and hurts enemies, while suffering no harm himself. For a woman it's tending to the home and children, and remaining true to her husband. Likewise I could describe virtue for a child, an old man, a slave, a free man...anyone you'd like. If you have no virtue, you have no Athens!

SOCRATES. I asked for one virtue, and he gives me a swarm! Suppose, Meno, that I ask you what a bee is, that is, what qualities make up a bee?

MENO. There are many types of bees.

32

SOCRATES. Exactly! Yes, exactly! Meaning they can be of different sorts and still be bees.

MENO. I don't—

SOCRATES. In other words, can these various species of bees, if you will, differ from one another in qualities all bees still have, such as size, color, or the strength of their stings?

MENO. They can differ in qualities all bees still have.

SOCRATES. While they are similar in qualities exclusive to bees.

MENO. Of course.

SOCRATES. And if we took the time, we could list the similarities, couldn't we?

MENO. I suppose.

SOCRATES. Common traits and habits that make them all still bees: nesting in hives, production of honey, what you will.

MENO. Of course.

SOCRATES. Then do the same with virtue. You say it's definitively central to Athens. But what makes virtue the same in an Athenian woman as in an Athenian man? The same in a citizen as a slave?

MENO. Virtue consists of a man directing the city well and a woman directing her household well. Perhaps it is the ability to govern others!

SOCRATES. Perhaps?

MENO. This is virtue.

SOCRATES. So a slave is virtuous who governs his master? A child who governs his parents?

The group laughs and jeers.

MENO. Of course not.

SOCRATES. And I have another problem. Shouldn't we add "justly" when we speak of how our virtuous person governs? Or is a tyrant virtuous? For certainly a tyrant governs others.

More guffawing.

MENO. We should add "justly," because… Ahah! Justice is virtue.

SOCRATES. Virtue, or A virtue?

MENO. Virtue, A virtue… what's the difference?

SOCRATES. Take roundness. Do we say it is "shape" or "A shape"?

MENO. Very well. There are virtues other than justice.

SOCRATES. And can you name them the way you can other shapes?

MENO. Dignity. Temperance. Wisdom.

SOCRATES. And of course here we are again: many virtues when we're looking for the one.

MENO. Obviously I can't give you what you want, Socrates.

The group responds, but Socrates quiets them.

SOCRATES. Let's try. If I take the example just now, and ask "what is shape," you'd say, as you did, roundness is "A shape" and not "shape."

MENO. I would.

SOCRATES. And when pressed you'd name other shapes.

MENO. Yes.

SOCRATES. And the same with, say, color. We can name white, black, red, and green, but doing so doesn't tell us what color is. In the question of shape we want to know that though one might be round, another square, one straight-edged, and another curved: What embraces them all that affixes to them this one word "shape"?

MENO. Yes.

SOCRATES. Then do your best to answer.

MENO. Why?

SOCRATES. As practice for finding a single definition of virtue!

MENO. Why don't you define shape, Socrates?

PLATO. *(To the Boy.)* Often he got so far ahead of us, he had to answer his own questions…

SOCRATES. If I do, will you give us the answer about virtue?

MENO. Sure.

SOCRATES. Shape is that sole thing that always accompanies color. Define virtue in this way and I'll be satisfied.

MENO. But I don't accept your definition.

SOCRATES. Because?

MENO. I don't yet know what color is.

Plato again to the Boy:

PLATO. And he was so quick he could do from many angles what the rest of us couldn't do from one...

SOCRATES. If I define shape again then, without using the word color, you'll tell me what virtue is?

MENO. Assuredly.

SOCRATES. Do you know what an end is, as in a boundary?

MENO. I do.

SOCRATES. And what about the words "surface" and "solid," as learned in our geometry?

MENO. These too.

SOCRATES. Shape then is that area inside of which a solid or surface meets its boundary.

MENO. But what is color?

SOCRATES. You're a lying scoundrel, Meno. You promise an old man you'll tell him what virtue is—

MENO. I will as soon as you tell us what color is.

SOCRATES. That's a promise?

MENO. Yes.

SOCRATES. Do you know what sight is, then?

MENO. I do.

SOCRATES. Color is the physical reality of shapes as they are perceptible to sight.

Meno turns to the crowd.

MENO. This is an excellent answer!

The crowd agrees. Socrates quiets them.

SOCRATES. We're in pursuit of something here. Truth, not praise! Meno: You say there's no Athens without virtue, so once more it's time for you to tell us about it. And stop separating the one into the many as if smashing plates!

MENO. It's too much, Socrates! You're too much! Please!

Socrates to the dikastai:

SOCRATES. Since many of you were children, people have whispered about me. "Socrates twists what is true to make the weaker argument the stronger and the stronger the weaker. He bewitches people, wishing a kind of anarchy by tormenting them with questions he himself can't answer. He is arrogant. Pompous. A bully. A pestilence." Have I summarized accurately? Let me begin with what you'll consider a boastful claim, but please know it wasn't I who first made it. You remember my friend Chaerephon, an ally to us all in ridding Athens of the tyrants just a few years ago.

> *A tired Xanthippe, the young and venerable wife of Socrates, greets Chaerephon, forties, exhausted.*

XANTHIPPE. Chaerephon...?!

CHAEREPHON. Your husband.

XANTHIPPE. What about my husband?

CHAEREPHON. Is he home?

XANTHIPPE. And asleep. As was I.

CHAEREPHON. You must wake him.

XANTHIPPE. It can't wait until morning?

CHAEREPHON. It's essential.

XANTHIPPE. Sleep is essential.

CHAEREPHON. Then go back to sleep after you wake him, woman.

> *Xanthippe leaves, then returns with a torch, lighting wall sconces. Socrates, in his forties, follows.*

SOCRATES. Would you like some food?

CHAEREPHON. Yes.

SOCRATES. *(To Xanthippe.)* Bread. And water. *(To Chaerephon.)* You're shaking. *(To Xanthippe.)* Some wine too.

> *Xanthippe leaves.*

So from where are you—?

CHAEREPHON. Delphi.

SOCRATES. Yes. You never told me why.

CHAEREPHON. I wasn't interested in your ridicule.

SOCRATES. I never ridicule.

CHAEREPHON. Let's not debate that right now. Do you believe what the Priestess says, Socrates?

SOCRATES. I neither believe nor disbelieve, having never been to her myself.

Xanthippe reappears with wine, water, and bread.

XANTHIPPE. Would you sit, Chaerephon? Please.

He does. Xanthippe pours wine.

CHAEREPHON. I've asked the Priestess certain questions.

SOCRATES. Go on.

CHAEREPHON. Pertaining to you.

SOCRATES. Why pertaining to me?

CHAEREPHON. I asked, Is there any man wiser than Socrates?

Socrates laughs.

SOCRATES. *(To Xanthippe.)* Do you hear this?

XANTHIPPE. What don't I hear?

SOCRATES. I'm not wise. I couldn't even tell you what wisdom is!

CHAEREPHON. The Priestess says there is no one wiser in Athens or all of Greece.

SOCRATES. Chaerephon—

CHAEREPHON. And I intend to let what your friends have known for years be known by everyone, which is that you have the mark of the deity on you.

SOCRATES. Chaerephon, why would you do such a thing?

CHAEREPHON. To protect you from harm.

SOCRATES. What is harm?

CHAEREPHON. I'm not debating definitions with you now either.

SOCRATES. What is harm to you?

CHAEREPHON. When others wish one ill, and act upon those wishes.

SOCRATES. I see.

CHAEREPHON. What, Socrates?

SOCRATES. If this is what you would spare me, Chaerephon, I fear you have done the opposite…

Socrates addresses the dikastai.

How did I respond to this, forgive me, but absurd claim by the Priestess imputing me to be the wisest man in Athens? First, I forbade Chaerephon and my wife from telling anyone what Chaerephon said he'd learned. Then my life from that moment, I swear to you, became devoted to proving the Priestess wrong. For understand this if you understand nothing else: I have never claimed to be wise. I've sought only goodness and truth. Wisdom, something utterly remote to me, never entered into it. I went immediately among you, and have not since relented, seeking in simple discourse with you, the citizens of Athens, the vast knowledge I still know myself not to possess.

> *Socrates, barefoot and unwashed as ever, trailed by two youths and a few men, approaches Thrasymachus, regal and well-heeled.*

THRASYMACHUS. Socrates. What brings you to the law courts?

SOCRATES. Believe it or not, Thrasymachus, I was looking for you.

THRASYMACHUS. I'm sorry but I've got to be inside. Some of us have actual responsibilities.

SOCRATES. And are to be praised for their dispatch. But we've walked half the city, including your own nephew.

> *Thrasymachus spies one of the youths.*

THRASYMACHUS. Aenesidemos, does my brother know you're following him around?

SOCRATES. Is keeping company with me somehow injurious to the boy?

THRASYMACHUS. My brother might think so, if solely for the havoc it's wreaking on the inside of the lad's nose.

SOCRATES. You seem to agree with your brother.

THRASYMACHUS. I've heard of your game, Socrates. Scuttling around Athens with this little audience, pestering everyone you meet.

SOCRATES. The building has yet to open. Please.

THRASYMACHUS. No.

SOCRATES. I beg you.

AENESIDEMOS. Please Uncle.

THRASYMACHUS. Briefly then.

SOCRATES. It's very simple: I've been teasing out a notion, or rather my lack of a notion, of something important to us all, and thought of no one more suitable than you, my most sapient friend, to help us. In a word, what is wisdom?

THRASYMACHUS. What is what?

SOCRATES. Wisdom?

THRASYMACHUS. We're finished here.

SOCRATES. Please sir. There's no leader more respected in Athens. You're elected to office whenever your name comes up. You counsel others as to how to speak, act, and even vote. You've led troops, donated and manned ships for the navy, hosted festivals for tens of thousands. A regular man of the people.

THRASYMACHUS. I needn't be reminded of my standing.

SOCRATES. Which you consider well deserved.

THRASYMACHUS. Your words, not mine.

SOCRATES. So?

THRASYMACHUS. Why don't YOU tell us what wisdom is.

SOCRATES. That's just the thing. Every time I think I know, the concept slips away.

　　　　Pause.

THRASYMACHUS. Wisdom is a kind of knowledge.

SOCRATES. Now already that makes sense. What kind of knowledge?

THRASYMACHUS. A deep kind that allows for the advising of other men.

SOCRATES. Yes! And thus you who are considered most wise advise, and Athens benefits! True?

THRASYMACHUS. Of course it's true.

SOCRATES. This is why we've sought you out! A few questions, to make sure I understand.

THRASYMACHUS. Socrates—

SOCRATES. Humor a man impaired by a deficiency of knowledge. For example, here in Athens only male citizens—those whose parents were both citizen born—can advise the city. Would you have it therefore that the wise can be discovered only within this group? In other words, can a woman, a noncitizen, a slave, a metic, or even a child be wise?

THRASYMACHUS. I see what you're doing Socrates, and of course. Those who are not citizens can advise others who are not. Likewise wise women advise other women, wise slaves other slaves.

SOCRATES. So wisdom is the ability to counsel others like to one's self.

THRASYMACHUS. If you will.

SOCRATES. And what of those who are counseled and do not counsel? Can they not be wise?

THRASYMACHUS. The wise needn't be counseled. They are wise.

SOCRATES. Do you seek counsel?

THRASYMACHUS. Rarely, if ever.

SOCRATES. But isn't it wise sometimes to listen rather than speak?

A pause.

THRASYMACHUS. I suppose it is.

SOCRATES. So it's not just advisors who are wise within a given group, but sometimes those who are advised.

THRASYMACHUS. Yes.

SOCRATES. And can it not be wise for a woman to be advised by a man, and likewise a man to be advised by a woman, should one or the other have more knowledge regarding a particular subject, skill, or task?

THRASYMACHUS. Yes.

SOCRATES. Meaning then that wisdom need not confine itself in terms of its transfer within a specific class, age, or sex.

Thrasymachus understands that his definition has now crumbled.

THRASYMACHUS. Right.

SOCRATES. Just a bit more.

THRASYMACHUS. I have little patience left.

SOCRATES. Please sir, lest I escape through the doors of your school not having learned.

THRASYMACHUS. Do not mock me Socrates.

SOCRATES. Mock you when I would learn from you? Would you have it that the advisors to a tyrant, say to Xerxes, those who counsel that he sow murder and destruction wherever his armies go, would you call such men wise?

THRASYMACHUS. Of course not.

SOCRATES. Or Xerxes for listening to them?

THRASYMACHUS. The advisors advise poorly, the other listens mistakenly.

SOCRATES. So we're learning then that far from being simply the ability to advise others similar to oneself, wisdom attaches both to those who counsel and choose to be counseled, no matter the sex, age, or station, but only to those who do so, shall we say, wisely.

THRASYMACHUS. Exactly.

SOCRATES. Wisdom then, according to the widely respected Thrasymachus of Athens, is defined…by what is wise?

> *Laughter.*

THRASYMACHUS. I know what wisdom is: understanding when to be quit of you. Come Aenesidemos.

AENESIDEMOS. I want to stay! It's incredible!

THRASYMACHUS. You're not staying!

> *Thrasymachus yanks the boy to his side. To Socrates:*

Keep away from me, and keep away from this boy!

> *Plato and the Boy.*

PLATO. All over Athens. But not just with leaders considered wise. Everyone! For who knew where actual truth might be discovered, or the lack of it exposed?

> *Socrates and his swelling group behold the poet Meletus the Elder (grandfather of the accuser of the same name).*

MELETUS THE ELDER.
> If to be rich with all its money
> meant one would never die,

I'd devote my life to earning,
and then when death strolled by,

I'd fill his hands with riches.
But there's no way to spend
to vanquish what time portends.
So since my days must end,

what good does a fortune do me,
or why then should I scorn
the certainty of dying
which comes when one is born?

My wealth piles up in friendship,
and quaffing wine at ease,
at nocturnal celebrations
of Love's eternities!

Socrates and his group applaud.

SOCRATES. Very engaging, Meletus. In both delivery and form.

Meletus the Elder bows.

MELETUS THE ELDER. But a work in progress. A good deal more to come.

SOCRATES. Just a few questions so we can learn something of the poetic art, and how it is deployed.

MELETUS THE ELDER. I am at your service. So long as you know these skills are rare. There is after all a reason we poets enjoy a fame in Athens equal to that of politicians and generals.

SOCRATES. I'll summon my courage. But why do you think that is, this exalted status?

MELETUS THE ELDER. We discover truths others don't see.

SOCRATES. As evidenced by recitations such as the one we just witnessed.

MELETUS THE ELDER. The poem and its recitation, yes.

SOCRATES. And these truths, they occur throughout the work, meaning it's devoid of the sorts of vagaries and falsehoods that litter common speech.

MELETUS THE ELDER. It's precisely this that makes it poetry.

SOCRATES. A blessing for Athens indeed. May I then speak back to you what I take your poem to mean?

MELETUS THE ELDER. Please.

SOCRATES. You seem to say that were death somehow vulnerable to bribe, whereby in paying him money one could live forever—

MELETUS THE ELDER. Well right there Socrates, I never spoke of immortality, which of course is reserved for the Gods.

SOCRATES. Then how am I to take "if one would never die"?

MELETUS THE ELDER. What's meant is a postponement.

SOCRATES. Clearly I'm stuck on the phrase "never die."

MELETUS THE ELDER. A certain license is not only tolerated, but expected in service of the art.

SOCRATES. Forgive me then as I tend to burrow into the meaning of things precisely as they are spoken, particularly given the afore-mentioned access to obscure and deeper truths that only poets would seem to enjoy. It will serve neither of us if I restrain this impulse. Would you agree?

MELETUS THE ELDER. As you wish.

SOCRATES. To continue then in your sense: Could you somehow bribe death into its postponement…

MELETUS THE ELDER. Yes.

SOCRATES. You'd gladly spend your life earning what it would take to do so.

MELETUS THE ELDER. Exactly.

SOCRATES. But since death cannot be so persuaded, you'll not squander time chasing drachmae, but instead will pursue life's true riches: friendship, wine, and celebrations of Love.

MELETUS THE ELDER. Socrates, you reveal not only your keen-ness as a listener, but the poem's clarity, especially when so pristinely delivered.

SOCRATES. No doubt. But tell us then, what is death?

MELETUS THE ELDER. Death is the end of life.

SOCRATES. All of life?

MELETUS THE ELDER. It's what's in store for us once we're born, as I say in the poem, placing death and birth in the same line I might add, exemplifying the kind of deeper poetic essence of which I was speaking. Birth leads to death: a juxtaposition of opposites—oxymoron would be the term of art—within a single couplet, a turn the common mind wouldn't ever conceive.

SOCRATES. Quite clever. But again, what is it?

MELETUS THE ELDER. What is what?

SOCRATES. Death.

MELETUS THE ELDER. I don't understand.

SOCRATES. Surely you must know something of its nature, if such extremes as avoiding all life's pleasures would be worth its postponement.

MELETUS THE ELDER. I don't know what awaits us in death. No one does.

SOCRATES. So could we even say it's just as likely death's to be embraced as feared?

MELETUS THE ELDER. I'm not going to say that.

SOCRATES. Why not?

MELETUS THE ELDER. Because everyone fears death.

SOCRATES. Everyone?

MELETUS THE ELDER. Almost everyone.

SOCRATES. The overwhelming majority.

MELETUS THE ELDER. If you will.

SOCRATES. And you are no doubt right. But if you, poet and seeker of truth, saw a dog on the Agora and wanted to approach it, its owner nowhere in sight, would you canvass those randomly near—passersby if you will, strangers like you to the animal—as to whether it were safe, or would you seek its owner for advice as to the canine's temperament?

MELETUS THE ELDER. I'd seek its owner.

SOCRATES. Why then do you trust the majority, those who, like you, know nothing of death, to instruct you as to its nature?

MELETUS THE ELDER. Because there is no owner of death as there is of the dog. No available expert on the subject. To extend your little parable, I choose not to pet the animal!

The audience chortles. Meletus the Elder bows theatrically.

SOCRATES. But that isn't what your poem says. Instead, you'd occupy your entire life fleeing from the dog if you could.

MELETUS THE ELDER. My poem is not about a dog on the Agora!

SOCRATES. It might as well be, for in each case you seem completely unacquainted with your subject.

MELETUS THE ELDER. You're telling me you don't fear death?

SOCRATES. Why should I fear what I know so little about?

MELETUS THE ELDER. Precisely for that reason.

SOCRATES. No, Meletus. For that reason I should pursue it.

MELETUS THE ELDER. Why don't you explain the poem?!

SOCRATES. I'm not its author.

Meletus the eventual accuser steps forward.

MELETUS. Have you ever written a poem, Socrates?

SOCRATES. I haven't.

MELETUS. A play? Anything?

SOCRATES. I don't write.

MELETUS. It's very easy to tear down my grandfather when you create nothing yourself.

SOCRATES. I'm not tearing him down. I'm simply pursuing the truths he and his poem claim exclusively to fathom.

MELETUS. Your hateful ridicule is not welcome here!

Socrates addresses the dikastai and gestures to Meletus.

SOCRATES. His grandfather a poet to be sure, his verse in certain respects commendable. But when really examined, it had no more meaning than plain speech—less even, for pretending truths it didn't possess. Was the process by which I discovered such falsity unfair, unkind, even humiliating? Perhaps. But the arrogance and pretense in the face of my search left me no choice. I began to conclude that perhaps the Priestess was right; for in understanding that I had so little wisdom, I could actually be wiser than our great poets and statesmen who claimed they had all of it. I suddenly

45

wondered: Was there a place with more deluded people than my own city? Our self-importance when it came to knowledge, both as individuals and as a society, was maddening beyond words.

Megasthenes, a forger of metals, sturdy and in his sixties, appears. He works a coal fire.

In desperation, I turned to our skilled craftsmen, realizing of course that though the son of a sculptor, I have few such skills myself.

Socrates, this time on his own, draws near.

MEGASTHENES. The ore comes from the mines in Elba, and it's carted here in chunks…

He points.

Mostly of that size. My father learned from his father, and the Mycenaeans were forging well before us, and in much the same way, which makes it a wonder we ever beat them in battle. Hah!

He shifts a tool inside the domed furnace.

The pieces lie there until they soften, which you can tell by the change of color.

He compresses a bellows, angering the flames.

We call this the tuyere. It blows the elements inside to let it breathe and grow livid. The slag will fall there to the bottom, leaving us iron. You see the holes?

Socrates stoops for a better look.

That's how you know. There's the bloom. Step aside. And mind your bare feet. Are you an idiot?

Socrates backs away as Megasthenes moves to a work area and begins hammering metal.

I'll pound this into some poor hoplite's cuirass and hope it'll hold against a Spartan spear. Hah! If the Gods will it, I'll have done my part.

SOCRATES. Do you support the war?

MEGASTHENES. Voted for it in the Assembly. You?

SOCRATES. I've fought. Was two years on the peninsula, including the retreat, and saw hundreds slaughtered; held dying men in my arms.

MEGASTHENES. That's not an answer.

SOCRATES. I'm a citizen of Athens, but her politics are little of my concern.

MEGASTHENES. You didn't hear what Pericles said?

SOCRATES. Remind me.

MEGASTHENES. "A man who takes no interest in politics isn't minding his own business; he has no business in Athens at all." Politics are your duty.

SOCRATES. You mind the business of Athens?

MEGASTHENES. I should rule Athens.

SOCRATES. How would you rule?

MEGASTHENES. I'm not worthy?

SOCRATES. I didn't say that.

MEGASTHENES. I've built more of these breastplates than I could count, as well as spears, daggers, and fittings of every shape for our ships.

SOCRATES. And so?

MEGASTHENES. I'm better equipped and more deserving to rule than any of these rich boys who skip the ranks because their fathers lease out slaves, or sell figs across the border, and can afford to buy them their station.

SOCRATES. Would you rule justly?

MEGASTHENES. I'd rule to make Athens great. That's what's just. Hah! Our system of government and way of life are the envy of the world. Let everyone bow down to us with thanks and call it what you want. You spoke earlier of the war. My son was at Sybota.

SOCRATES. I wasn't aware.

MEGASTHENES. Speared by a Corinthian through the stomach. Back then it was a different kind of fighting at sea. They fought hand to hand on the decks as if it were land. He went overboard, drowning in seawater mixed with his own blood, as it was described to me. My only son. What was it to me or him that Corcyra no longer wanted to be ruled by Corinth? And yet we sent our sons and our ships, and started a war with Sparta that seems like it'll never end. And here I still am, hammering weapons and breast-plates for it, though it cost me my family line. Men will rule other men. It's what we want.

SOCRATES. But given the choice, would you have just rule or unjust?

MEGASTHENES. Just, I suppose.

SOCRATES. And who prevails in war?

MEGASTHENES. The side that kills more of the other.

SOCRATES. With all this equipment you've hammered.

MEGASTHENES. That's right.

SOCRATES. Do we say killing is just or do we condemn it?

MEGASTHENES. That depends.

SOCRATES. As a rule.

MEGASTHENES. We condemn it, moron.

SOCRATES. Then why would you have something we condemn determine who rules, and even go so far as to call it just?

MEGASTHENES. I'm an Athenian! We fight because the Assembly votes for it!

SOCRATES. And so says everyone in Athens.

MEGASTHENES. As well they should!

SOCRATES. But does that mean the Assembly is always right? Including sending your only son into battle?

>   *Megasthenes stares in silence.*

And am I to take it therefore that it was right and just and good that your son was killed?

>   *Megasthenes lunges, taking Socrates by his cloak. He throws*
>   *him to the ground and begins to pummel and kick him*
>   *savagely. Others join the beating.*

PLATO. *(To the Boy.)* There were attempts to drown him, set him on fire. No matter. Nothing would stop him. Wherever he encountered ignorance behind the pretense of wisdom, he challenged it. Wisdom, he told the jury...

>   *Socrates rises from the beating to address the dikastai.*

SOCRATES. ...is the property of the Gods, and the wisest among us knows that in respect to wisdom he is utterly worthless!

PLATO. Soon no one was better known, which made him all the more despised, because the powerful—especially in Athens—want more than anything to be recognized, and he had that without even striving for it.

Socrates addresses Plato.

SOCRATES. Would that I weren't known.

PLATO. I asked him why.

SOCRATES. Now to argue with me is a sport. Can I best Socrates?

PLATO. *(To the Boy.)* The divide widened between those who loathed and those who admired him, with no one in between; the latter mostly the young of course, and the former their parents, grandparents, aunts, uncles. His followers—he forbade us calling ourselves his students—

BOY. Why?

Plato doesn't answer, waits.

Because that would mean he had knowledge, which of course he was claiming he didn't. That's why you couldn't call him a teacher.

PLATO. We began to imitate him, questioning all that our parents held true, turning every interaction into a kind of game, the cleverest among us, to escape the hypocrisy of authority. "How can you tell me what I've done is wrong when you can't even define for me what is right," I once said to my father. "Why don't you tell me what is right then," he answered. To which I of course responded, "I'm not the one claiming to know." Imagine the seething rage of all the fathers subjected to that. This won't, by the way, be the nature of our arrangement.

BOY. I didn't think so.

PLATO. But none hated him more than those who used the trickery of words in the public sphere, for it was this pursuit he himself most despised: The more wisdom you claimed in pursuit of power over others, the more he wanted to disabuse you. One of the most famous was an old sophist visiting from Leontini named Gorgias. It was arranged Socrates would meet him at the house of a mean, bitter man named Callicles, who had invited others.

Gorgias, old and brilliant, stands opposite Socrates. Callicles and Chaerephon listen, along with half a dozen others, including the eventual accuser Anytus, and Polus.

Plato and the Boy join.

SOCRATES. *(Points to Polus.)* Your friend Polus here keeps giving speeches. Are you willing to refrain from such lecturing?

GORGIAS. Unless you ask questions that demand long answers!

    Laughter.

SOCRATES. You trade in the ability to persuade others, which you call rhetoric.

GORGIAS. Yes.

SOCRATES. Help understand more precisely. Just what is rhetoric? With what does it concern itself?

GORGIAS. Words.

SOCRATES. Words of what sort?

GORGIAS. Any sort.

SOCRATES. Your brother is a doctor I'm told.

GORGIAS. He is.

SOCRATES. Those your brother would use to diagnose an illness?

GORGIAS. Yes, but not solely.

SOCRATES. A mathematician to describe a sum?

GORGIAS. Rhetoric is the art of ALL words. There's nothing it doesn't touch, which is why again I submit that, particularly in a democracy, it is the noblest of all pursuits.

SOCRATES. Leaving democracy aside for the moment, couldn't a doctor say the same? That he looks after the health of his patients, and there's no greater boon than health? Or a trainer who maintains the fitness of our bodies? Or even a merchant who earns enough to bring food, shelter, and warmth to friends and kin?

GORGIAS. They might.

SOCRATES. What would you say back?

GORGIAS. I've said it already, have I not? Rhetoric encompasses these and all areas.

SOCRATES. To make sure I understand: If the subject were say the building of walls or temples, would we be best to consult the rhetorician along with builders, masons, and architects?

GORGIAS. Your docks and walls were designed from the advice of Themistocles, were they not? Pericles conceived the building of the middle wall.

SOCRATES. All true.

GORGIAS. You mentioned my brother. I've been with him when patients would refuse a treatment—say the taking of medicine or the cauterizing of a wound, and would you believe it was I, solely with rhetoric, who could persuade them? With enough information, put an orator up against a specialist, and the orator will speak more effectively every time.

SOCRATES. I believe it, but in front of what sort of audience?

GORGIAS. Any audience.

SOCRATES. Surely not experts on a topic, for they would know enough to prefer a specialist.

   Pause.

GORGIAS. In certain cases. That I can grant you.

SOCRATES. Meaning really that when it comes to rhetoric, the ignorant can be more persuasive than the knowledgeable, but mostly before an audience of the ignorant.

GORGIAS. I wouldn't put it that way.

SOCRATES. No, in fact it could be argued, Gorgias, that your rhetoric depends on such an imbalance, and the more ignorant the audience the better.

GORGIAS. As I said—I keep having to repeat myself with you— that's not how I'd put it.

SOCRATES. How would you put it?

GORGIAS. Simply that, especially here in Athens where most topics are decided upon by vote, rhetoric is more prized than any other skill.

SOCRATES. Yes, you mentioned that. But what startles me is that we seem to be determining that in a democracy it's more useful to speak effectively than to know about a subject.

ANYTUS. This is how you'd characterize democracy, Socrates?

SOCRATES. It is how Gorgias characterizes democracy.

ANYTUS. Gorgias spoke of rhetoric.

SOCRATES. And its place in our democracy. He introduced the word, not I. Am I wrong?

Polus interjects, eager to defuse the growing tension.

POLUS. Why don't you tell us, Socrates, what sort of art YOU think rhetoric to be?

SOCRATES. Will that suit our good friend Anytus?

ANYTUS. I'm eager to hear.

SOCRATES. I liken it to cooking.

POLUS. How so?

SOCRATES. Cooking pleases and gratifies, does it not?

POLUS. Potentially.

SOCRATES. But put a doctor and a cook in front of an average person, and have them concoct a meal from what they consider the best foods, who would be likely to persuade the eater his was the better choice?

POLUS. The cook I suppose.

SOCRATES. Though the doctor's would no doubt be the healthier.

POLUS. Probably.

SOCRATES. Your rhetorician then is to the soul as the cook is to the body. Gratifying in the moment, but seldom better or for the good.

ANYTUS. So now Athenians are ignorant?

SOCRATES. There seems to be a problem here. As before, I never mentioned Athenians, Anytus, you did.

ANYTUS. By likening our politicians to cooks using delightful flavors.

SOCRATES. How would you characterize our politicians?

ANYTUS. As those best equipped to inform and lead.

SOCRATES. And yours is the popular opinion, but answer me if you would, for this speaks directly to what troubles me.

ANYTUS. Happily.

SOCRATES. Insofar as rhetoricians go, one would want most to learn from them how to give speeches and persuade others, as Gorgias describes.

ANYTUS. Correct.

SOCRATES. But should you need, say, to build a ship—not speak about the building of it, but actually build it—would you go to Gorgias for the design, or a shipbuilder?

ANYTUS. A shipbuilder.

SOCRATES. And for plans to erect a bridge, an architect or Polus here?

ANYTUS. An architect.

SOCRATES. I'd seek out you if I had hides that needed treating.

ANYTUS. Leave me out of it.

SOCRATES. I'm simply curious why do we not do the same when it comes to Athens, and let those best fit to lead lead, rather than the ones who give the most entertaining speeches, largely to the uninformed, or even worse, are chosen by lottery rather than because they're qualified?

ANYTUS. The lottery is a foundation of our democracy.

SOCRATES. Does that make it best?

ANYTUS. It most certainly does.

SOCRATES. Why? Because you've hauled in the sacred word "democracy" in defense of it, a word by the way that anyone can use, and I'm meant to cower?

CHAEREPHON. Socrates…

ANYTUS. Chaerephon, don't interrupt.

SOCRATES. We have a system that puts citizens in charge based on their names being drawn from an urn, and not their worthiness, and decisions made by voters not informed by learning or study, but because they've heard a blustery speech filled with keen rhetoric and silly promises.

ANYTUS. Now we're to the heart of it.

SOCRATES. Let us hope.

CHAEREPHON. Socrates, please...

ANYTUS. CHAEREPHON!

Silence.

Would you tear down our democracy?

SOCRATES. Not by any means.

ANYTUS. The greatest system for governing that man has ever devised. For which countless Athenians have given their lives? For which we've endured nothing less than starvation, war, and then tyranny.

SOCRATES. I speak not of the tyrants nor of history.

ANYTUS. Of course you won't speak of the tyrants. You taught them how to tyrannize, every one.

SOCRATES. I recall the Spartans installing the tyrants as a term of our surrender, Anytus, not I.

ANYTUS. Like Alcibiades, the tyrants were students of yours, all. You'll now deny you taught them?

SOCRATES. I've taught no one anything. And I am not a political man.

ANYTUS. You're not?

SOCRATES. Have I sought high office? Nor will I ever, not being worthy. Every time my name comes up I fight the appointment.

ANYTUS. Yet you harass our leaders relentlessly and publicly, day after day, claiming they're unfit.

SOCRATES. When do I claim anything? I simply ask questions. And these leaders. Do we choose the best among us for the task? If not, why? And should we blame the leaders for that, or those who vote for them? Or the system itself?

ANYTUS. Socrates...

SOCRATES. Is this not Athens, where I may speak and question as I choose?

ANYTUS. Not in ways that challenge the state that gives you that right.

SOCRATES. Who's more dangerous to your democracy, Anytus, you or I?

ANYTUS. Be very careful Socrates.

SOCRATES. I question falsehood in any form, and the presumption of knowledge where there is none, most of all within myself. If it's such falsehoods you and others hold dear, no matter the arena, no matter the topic, no matter the status of the man, be assured, I'll do all in my power to tear them down.

ANYTUS. You would now tear me down?

POLUS. Gentlemen, please.

ANYTUS. Step back Polus.

Polus does so.

Who are you to say what's false and what's true?

SOCRATES. Who is anyone? Let us search together.

ANYTUS. I will protect Athens.

SOCRATES. A noble goal, and mine as well.

ANYTUS. Your goal is the well-being of Socrates.

SOCRATES. Above all else.

ANYTUS. I thank you Callicles for including me today. Athens has heard from you Socrates. Soon you will hear from Athens.

Plato and Socrates.

SOCRATES. You sound like my wife.

PLATO. Is that a bad thing?

SOCRATES. Depends on the day. Or lately the hour.

PLATO. And if charges are brought and you're tried? Publicly?

SOCRATES. How else would I be tried in this confoundingly ridiculous city I so love? It would resemble a doctor being judged by pastry cooks before a jury of children.

PLATO. With a verdict all the same.

SOCRATES. And what would be the charge? Pursuing ideas?

PLATO. This is Athens. Any charge you like; it wouldn't have to have a thing to do with whatever hatefulness lay behind it.

SOCRATES. And based on what evidence? The writing you've been doing?

A pause.

PLATO. I'm sorry?

SOCRATES. Have you been writing?

Silence.

PLATO. I always write.

SOCRATES. What I say.

Pause.

PLATO. Who told you?

SOCRATES. Crito.

PLATO. Crito encourages it.

SOCRATES. He informed Xanthippe.

PLATO. Of course.

SOCRATES. Which conversations?

PLATO. Every conversation.

SOCRATES. If I meant for myself to be remembered like that—

PLATO. Which begs the obvious question...

SOCRATES. Writing distorts truth.

PLATO. Or brings clearer truth. When you are no longer here—

SOCRATES. Are you now a historian? You're a philosopher. We write words on the soul.

PLATO. Lucky indeed for anyone within earshot.

SOCRATES. Men can't know me by reading what I've said.

PLATO. But reading what you've said can still make them wise.

SOCRATES. Less wise.

PLATO. How can that be?

SOCRATES. In understanding what a table is, that is, exploring all aspects of a physical shape that makes the word "table" appropriate when affixed to it, what would you have me do, read a description or see the thing itself?

PLATO. See the thing itself of course. But if seeing the thing isn't possible—

SOCRATES. You'd have me read a description written by another.

PLATO. Or look at a painting. Or even see it AND read the description, adding texture to your understanding.

SOCRATES. More on that in a moment, and let's leave painting aside, for what I would tell you is that by reading about a thing, I might ultimately know less about its true nature than if I'd never seen or read about it at all.

PLATO. How?

SOCRATES. For being tricked into the misapprehension I had any understanding of what a table is without actually seeing one, causing me to be less zealous in my quest to learn about the actual thing.

PLATO. Why not more zealous, having been made curious?

SOCRATES. This has not been my experience of human nature. And in the case of seeing a table and then reading about it, I can suddenly take what is written—a set of external reminders—as the truth of the thing, rather than what I actually might recall. With writing, I am reminded, in other words, instead of actually having to remember. I weaken my mind rather than strengthening it. Doesn't this make me less wise?

PLATO. By possibly increasing your knowledge?

SOCRATES. By giving me the illusion of increasing my knowledge, when instead I'm depending on knowledge written down separate from me, most likely by someone else, and worse, by arrogantly feeling like I have some understanding of the thing when actually I don't, for either never having seen it, or having replaced seeing it by reading jottings on a scroll. I fear a time when all knowledge is outside of us, and we have nothing in our minds at all.

PLATO. Men won't stop writing.

SOCRATES. Nor will they cease murdering, making war, deceiving themselves and others.

PLATO. Now writing is akin to murder and war?

SOCRATES. I merely point out that the endurance and even prevalence of an action hardly justifies its use.

PLATO. I won't stop.

SOCRATES. When I die, what then?

PLATO. Will I stop writing?

SOCRATES. About me at the very least.

PLATO. I can't promise that.

SOCRATES. Your memory will change what I've said, mix it with your ideas as they differ from mine.

PLATO. They will not differ from yours.

SOCRATES. Can't you see? They already do.

Anytus, Meletus, Lycon, and others stand before the Archon.

ALL. We've been perfectly clear! This will go forward as prescribed! You'll do as the law demands!

ARCHON. SILENCE! The law courts are no place for personal vendettas! We're no longer under the tyrants, or have you forgotten?

LYCON. The death of a son?! My son!

ARCHON. There is supposed to be an amnesty, Lycon!

LYCON. I see…

ARCHON. And you cannot blame your son's execution on Socrates, certainly not before a jury. If I had something tangible.

ANYTUS. In your hand. Six charges when only one need suffice. Concrete, provable, and final.

The Archon looks at a scroll.

ARCHON. The Herms and Mysteries? More than a decade ago. And no one has ever connected either to Socrates.

ANYTUS. He and Alcibiades—

ARCHON. Were lovers? Denied by both men. Moreover, not a crime. If it were you could accuse half the men of Athens. The majority in this room would be exiled!

The Archon returns to the scroll.

Speaking out against the state? Please. I'll not bring it. Corrupts the youth? Which? Can you present them?

ANYTUS. Countless.

ARCHON. And they'd praise him, every one. My own bovine son included. You'd be laughed out of the building. *(Back to scroll.)*

Worships the wrong Gods? Prove he's impious. You can't. I'm sorry. We all want this, but we're still a city of laws, as Socrates will be the first to remind you, even if he ridicules them, every one.

ANYTUS. You will bring these charges, and we will have this trial.

ARCHON. You can say that as much as you like, Anytus—

ANYTUS. Bring it or we will draw up charges accusing you of protecting him.

ARCHON. You'll bring charges against me?

ANYTUS. He is the enemy of Athens.

ARCHON. You haven't proven that!

ANYTUS. Protect him and you too are an enemy.

ARCHON. Your charge against me would have no basis!

ANYTUS. Would you be brought before the assembly to defend yourself? Because I tell you we will do as I say.

ARCHON. Willfully lie?

ANYTUS. I ask again: Will you risk banishment or at the very least ruining your name and that of your family protecting a man you despise?

ARCHON. This is not how the law is meant to work!

ANYTUS. The law is for justice, and we will use the law as we see fit. For justice. To extinguish him. We want it, you want it, the citizens of Athens want it. It's time to let a jury decide. Let them tell us the charges have no merit. In this city the people rule!

    Plato and the Boy.

PLATO. Think of it. Charged for being an atheist, but also for worshipping the wrong Gods. How can an atheist believe in any God? By the simplest logic the two charges cannot coexist, but there they were, and listed consecutively to make it even more maliciously incoherent. Corrupting the youth? Far from ever touching a boy, he loathed that that went on here. But know this and know it always: In Athens, when the citizens want something, it will transpire. The many brutalize the one, the law itself making it so. Democracy with a vengeance. No one understood this better than Socrates. Just six years before his trial, the Assembly voted to seize the port at Mytilene and endeavor once again to crush the

Spartan fleet. We sent every ship, and thousands drowned. The city went mad with grief, desperate for men to blame. Who else but the six generals, and worse, to be tried as a group, not individually, against every custom we held dear. And only Socrates to defend the accused, as his name had been drawn from the urn.

> *A mob rages, barely containable, while Socrates stands apart, Crito interceding.*

MOB. They fled, leaving thousands to drown! No manner of storm should have caused their abandonment! The generals thought only of themselves! They must die, every one! No more speeches! We put it to a vote!

CRITO. Let him speak! We must let him speak!

SOCRATES. Thank you Crito. We don't condemn and try groups, but individuals on the merits of each case! These men will not be judged and sentenced in this way! You're playing with their lives!

LYCON. If the council wishes it we will!

SOCRATES. The council may wish all it likes, but I will not grant it! And you will hear me!

CRITO. We will hear him!

SOCRATES. Because that is the law! And if you don't want the law followed you should never have conscripted me as leader of this council against my will!

LYCON. You won't be leader tomorrow!

SOCRATES. Not soon enough! We've lost brothers, fathers, uncles, children! But we do not right such wrongs by rushing—

LYCON. WE DO!

> *The mob roars in support of Lycon.*

SOCRATES. BY RUSHING TO JUDGE WITHOUT LAWFUL TRIAL!! Each of them must be allowed to speak in his defense!

MOB. KILL THEM NOW! KILL THEM NOW! KILL THEM NOW!

> *The mob explodes in a frenzy.*

SOCRATES. AS THE LAW STATES! NOT THE MOB, BUT THE LAW!

A melee of rage, Socrates utterly alone.

PLATO. The next day, with Socrates removed, the vote went forward, and the six were condemned, victims of the city's enraged lament.

> *The six accused appear, lashed with iron cuffs to boards: an early "bloodless" crucifixion.*

Murdered publicly, one at a time, though they'd been tried as a group.

> *Soldiers step behind the boards and yank ropes around each neck of the accused, who writhe in unison as they are strangled to death.*

This was our Athens.

> *Socrates to the dikastai:*

SOCRATES. We have endured so very much. Perpetual war, starvation, recrimination, profound uncertainty, tyranny, and plague. And a kind of rage in this city the likes of which I have never seen. A democracy divided. And so here I stand: my turn before you, at least half of Athens it would seem wishing me killed. Yet, especially in such times, no one worth anything will waste energy worrying about death. The worthwhile person must consider only this: Do I act rightly, or wrongly? Am I a good man or bad? And were you to say to me right now, "Socrates, we'll let you go free, but you must stop philosophizing or face death," I would answer that I will not stop, but will keep pursuing, questioning everyone I meet, saying, "You, Athenian! Why do you seek wealth and power and every comfort, but refuse to ask what your life and the world around you might actually mean? What is true? And what is not true in this blessed life?" If doing so means to you that I corrupt our youth, or I'm an atheist, or worship the wrong Gods, so be it. As long as I live freely, I shall do just as I have done, no matter the mendacious accusations you affix to it. I will question relentlessly what we hold most sacred, what we live for, what we die for, even if it means I'm murdered a hundred times over.

> *He nods to the Archon, who steps forward.*

ARCHON. So concludes this phase of the trial of Socrates.

>*Two men carry a large urn to the center of the stage before the Archon.*

You have each been issued two discs.

>*He produces one, about two inches in diameter.*

A solid disc means guilty.

>*He shows another of identical size with a hole in the middle.*

A disc hollow in the center means innocent. You will place the disc signifying your vote in the urn.

End of Act One

ACT TWO

Plato and the Boy.

BOY. If the charges were so ridiculous—even contradictory—lies as you say—

PLATO. You doubt it?

BOY. As you describe them, no.

PLATO. It's not as I describe them, it's what they were. Which seems quite important to you by the way.

BOY. What's that?

PLATO. The facts of things.

BOY. Will that be a problem?

PLATO. I don't imagine so.

BOY. Otherwise how do we make sense of anything?

PLATO. I see.

BOY. You're smiling.

PLATO. Am I?

BOY. Why?

PLATO. Must we make sense of everything?

BOY. You don't think?

PLATO. Maybe I don't know if we can.

BOY. Don't we do it every day?

PLATO. How is that?

BOY. By giving names to animals and objects and actions, for instance.

PLATO. Categorizing?

BOY. I suppose that's a way of putting it.

PLATO. You suppose?

BOY. Or each city writes laws as to what can and can't be done. We organize activities based on the rising and setting and movement of the sun and the changing of seasons. We even have tragedies that instruct us how to live and think.

PLATO. You believe tragedies instruct us?

BOY. Is that not their aim?

PLATO. It certainly is. The question is, are we making sense of the world, or just fooling ourselves into thinking we have, thereby distancing ourselves from it even further? In a way like what he thought about writing, meaning the more we believe we have organized truths, the further away from them we actually get.

BOY. You're saying it's futile?

PLATO. Possibly. Maybe even hopefully.

BOY. Then what's the point of all this?

PLATO. Perhaps to live in a way that gets you as close as you can, though you know it's unlikely you'll ever get there. Does that make sense?

The Boy thinks.

BOY. I don't know.

PLATO. And you shouldn't.

BOY. But even given how so many despised him, couldn't he have spent more of his time answering the charges, instead of recounting the story of his life?

PLATO. It drove me crazy.

BOY. So?

PLATO. I can only tell you what I thought at the time. To have done so would have put saving himself first, meaning ahead of what his actions stood for. He wanted, in other words, to be voted innocent for who and what he was, not because of his dexterity at refuting charges.

BOY. But they were false. It would have been so easy.

PLATO. Should you embrace this life, there will come a moment when you too must decide whether to engage with the political system on its terms or not.

BOY. Why do I have to decide that?

PLATO. Either you will need it, or you'll come to believe that it needs you.

BOY. What need could any political system ever possibly have for me?

PLATO. You'll be surprised how useful a person like you can be. Better you than others anyway. Of course what was clear to all of us, most of all Socrates, was that by choosing so publicly to shun politics, he was engaging in politics more deeply and more dangerously than any of us. Moderation, or worse, very aggressively not to participate, meant making an enemy of everyone.

    Crito appears.

CRITO. Will he meet us?

PLATO. In the room where they're keeping him. Xanthippe is already there.

CRITO. They allowed her?

PLATO. You think she was going to let herself be barred?

    Plato and Crito move to where Socrates waits with Xanthippe.

SOCRATES. Welcome to you both. What shall we do while five hundred and one Solons decide the fate of such a simple and guileless man?

XANTHIPPE. You'll be quiet and listen.

SOCRATES. Even my wife wishes me silenced.

XANTHIPPE. Silent, not silenced.

CRITO. The point is to make sure you won't be killed.

SOCRATES. You're finding me guilty already.

PLATO. You're certainly not helping your cause.

SOCRATES. I thought I spoke well.

PLATO. Athenians don't want to be lectured to. Certainly not by you.

SOCRATES. Was I lecturing?

PLATO. It would seem.

SOCRATES. What do Athenians want?

PLATO. To know that if you remain here—

SOCRATES. Remain alive—

PLATO. Alive or in Athens—

SOCRATES. I'll keep quiet?

PLATO. Tell them what's true.

SOCRATES. And what is true in this instance?

PLATO. That you want to make their city stronger, not tear it down.

SOCRATES. Regarding our great city—for it is my city too—my concern is for the people as individuals, not as Athenians. This still hasn't occurred to Anytus and the others. Apparently not to you either.

PLATO. And are you better for those individuals dead or alive?

SOCRATES. I suppose that's, as you say, for the Athenians to decide.

CRITO. Perhaps the rest of us aren't so comfortable with your life in the hands of others...particularly those presently sitting in judgment.

SOCRATES. As I said—

XANTHIPPE. Please. For once.

SOCRATES. Continue, Crito.

CRITO. Should they find you guilty, you can at least convince them to let you live. If not for yourself, do it for us. For your family.

SOCRATES. Tell me what you want.

CRITO. Have Xanthippe appear. Present her with your children as is the custom.

SOCRATES. I won't allow my wife and boys to be gawped at by such a gathering, or I would have trotted them out there already.

XANTHIPPE. What if it's what I want?

SOCRATES. Neither you nor the children have anything to do with the charges, nor with proving that I have never wronged a soul.

XANTHIPPE. I can say what you won't.

SOCRATES. What could that possibly be?

XANTHIPPE. Pardon?

SOCRATES. I know you won't extoll my virtues as a husband and father, given the berating that goes on under my roof on a daily basis.

XANTHIPPE. A daily basis? You're home every day?

CRITO. I urge the two of you—

XANTHIPPE. He infuriates me.

SOCRATES. I hadn't noticed.

XANTHIPPE. I can speak of how you haven't taken money from a single person you've taught.

SOCRATES. I don't teach.

XANTHIPPE. That's complete nonsense. *(Gesturing to the others.)* Your little tricks might work with them, but not with me.

SOCRATES. Little tricks?

XANTHIPPE. Do you deny that others have learned from you?

SOCRATES. They think they have.

XANTHIPPE. Call it what you like, people, of every age and station, believe they learn from you. I've raised a family on nothing because you won't take money even when it's offered for what they perceive to be a service. The wealthiest of this city try to pour money on you. People with whom you've spent more time and to whom you've given far more of yourself than to your own wife and children. Most of them don't even know you have a family.

CRITO. It's true.

XANTHIPPE. Let them see us.

SOCRATES. No.

XANTHIPPE. Sir!

SOCRATES. The children will not appear. You will not appear.

He turns to Plato and Crito.

What else?

XANTHIPPE. Why did I even bother?

CRITO. Should you be found guilty, without your family for sympathy you have only one other option…

PLATO. *(To the Boy.)* We could barely lay it out by the time the discs were counted. We knew only that he'd heard our offer—not that he'd agreed to it—when word came the verdict would be read.

The Archon to the dikastai:

ARCHON. As pertains to the following claims: that Socrates has worshiped false Gods, that Socrates has practiced atheism, that Socrates has corrupted the youth of Athens…

He produces a small scroll.

Two hundred and sixty-five say guilty, two hundred and thirty-six say not guilty. Socrates has been found guilty by the Athenian people. The accusers have made their case for death. Should he choose, Socrates will now propose an alternate sentence. Neither this court nor the dikastai shall determine a third punishment. Following a second vote, Socrates will die, or suffer a fate he himself proposes.

He turns to Socrates.

Socrates, do you wish to address the dikastai?

SOCRATES. Thirty votes separate me from innocence. Just fifteen if we're to be mathematically precise. Had I had one accuser instead of three, I might have won.

Pause.

A punishment suitable.

He stares at his calloused, bare feet, scratches at his beard.

How have I spent my life? I have badgered people like the gadfly that keeps coming back to bite the horse. I have no power, no rank, no money. What to do with such a dangerous criminal who lives only to better himself and others, and has only a capital charge to show for it?

No answer.

You protect and feed him of course! I therefore propose that, like our Olympic victors, I be housed in the Prytaneum and fed by the state so that I can keep doing exactly what I'm doing!

Silence.

Ah. Perhaps that isn't what you had in mind. My friend Plato tells me I must show remorse. Should I be banished? No doubt you'd accept this, perhaps with some relief, so off I'd go at my age to torment other peoples, many of them your enemies, getting booted out of town after town for the same reasons you'd expel me from Athens: The young would follow me, and their elders despise me, which is to say nothing of the Gods I may or may not worship. And of course as with here I'd be blamed indiscriminately for the offenses of others. You could say why not live life quietly somewhere, and perhaps this is what is hardest to make you understand. For I tell you that to spend every day examining life, and yes, doing so publicly, is to me the only way to exist, and to cease doing so would make life simply not worth living. Why live at all without asking yourself and others how BEST to live? So finally there is the option of a fine.

Plato with the Boy.

PLATO. And there it was. I couldn't believe it. Had we actually convinced him?

BOY. He could have just paid a fine?

PLATO. Show real penance without forfeiture of his life. Spare the dikastai the inconvenience of his blood on their hands.

Socrates continues.

SOCRATES. What do I care for money, so giving it away would cause me no harm. But what can I afford? As everyone knows, I have very little.

He makes a show of calculating in his head.

One mina…nearly half of all I own. That I could manage. So there it is: a single mina to mighty Athens for my single paltry life!

PLATO. Socrates!

CRITO. Please!

OTHERS. No!

ARCHON. Citizens!

SOCRATES. Very well. Plato and Crito there and some of the others have offered thirty minae on their guarantee. I propose this sum as my punishment. A fortune such as I and most of you could never imagine. This should settle it!

Plato and the Boy.

PLATO. You could feel the relief in the room. The dikastai were all but thanking him. If he'd only done, in that moment, what he could never do…

BOY. Keep his mouth shut.

PLATO. Walk away. Know he had made his point and they theirs.

Socrates raises a finger.

SOCRATES. But know this, should it not be clear: As long as I live, by day and by night, wherever I may wander, I will challenge you and all you stand for that seems wicked and false. I will never cease the very behavior that has incensed so many! Not ever, so long as I breathe!

PLATO. Once more the dikastai voted.

ARCHON. By a margin of fifty-three the dikastai have determined thusly:

The Archon reads from a scroll.

Socrates is sentenced to death.

PLATO. In the end, more wished him dead than found him guilty.

ARCHON. This determination is final, and shall be carried out when the ships return from their annual pilgrimage to Delos.

Crito jeers, inspiring others to join. Socrates gestures to Anytus, Meletus, and Lycon.

SOCRATES. Pity them, not me. I go now to die, and you to live. Which of us will be the happier, only the God knows!

Plato to the Boy.

PLATO. And so the atheist invoking his unsanctioned God was taken to the cell where he was to die. But by an attenuating coincidence the law forbade that he be killed immediately. Ships were away on an annual pilgrimage, and no one was to be executed until their return.

Night. Crito with a torch.

Crito was at the port day and night.

Aetios, a ship captain, appears with a torch as well.

CRITO. Aetios.

AETIOS. Crito? What brings you down here?

CRITO. Waiting for anyone who's been at sea.

AETIOS. Of course. They made port at Sunium last night, and would have left this morning but needed provisions. I'm sorry.

CRITO. Welcome home.

Plato sits with Xanthippe, Eryximachus, an aristocrat named Cebes, and a Theban named Simmias.

SIMMIAS. Please trust me. Your husband will live out his days. Your sons will bury him, and raise children of their own, or return to Athens, should they choose.

Crito enters, out of breath.

CRITO. Simmias. What word from Thebes?

SIMMIAS. It's been arranged.

CRITO. *(To Xanthippe.)* And you've agreed?

XANTHIPPE. I'm not the one who'll need persuading.

PLATO. Where is the ship?

CRITO. Within a day.

XANTHIPPE. Please go now so you're there when he wakes.

Socrates' cell.
A chained Socrates sleeps. A guard rests nearby. Crito nudges him awake and hands over coins.

CRITO. Unshackle him and leave us.

Crito beholds Socrates.

How can he possibly...?

Socrates wakes as he's unfettered.

SOCRATES. Is it morning?

The guard leaves.

PLATO. Crito was wondering how you can sleep.

SOCRATES. I've spent my life preparing for death.

CRITO. That may be...

SOCRATES. It would hardly become a man my age to resent his own end, don't you think?

PLATO. That depends what you believe awaits you.

SOCRATES. Say I'm not certain.

PLATO. Then maybe a long and happy life unencumbered by sickness could just as easily compel a man to want to live.

SOCRATES. Meaning a healthy old man could actually lament dying more than a youth in his prime?

PLATO. Something like that.

Socrates sits up.

SOCRATES. Let's tease this out.

CRITO. Damn you both, and especially you Plato.

SOCRATES. The boat approaches.

CRITO. And we've just been with your wife.

SOCRATES. Who again begs me to agree to some kind of clemency.

CRITO. Better. Simmias has made arrangements for your escape to Thebes, and your protection and maintenance there.

SOCRATES. Thebes will do what Athens wouldn't.

CRITO. Yes.

SOCRATES. You mean to bribe the court?

PLATO. Already done.

CRITO. No one will blame you.

SOCRATES. Haven't we always held that popular opinion is largely to be ignored?

CRITO. Fine.

SOCRATES. So without wasting precious time, what others say shouldn't sway us one way or another.

CRITO. So long as we actually DO something.

SOCRATES. You're starting to agree with the jury that it's better I be put to death than having to listen to me anymore.

CRITO. A lot has to happen.

SOCRATES. But should we decide it's best I remain here, will I hear no more of this?

CRITO. Agreed.

SOCRATES. Answer me, both of you. Do we still believe one must never willingly do wrong?

PLATO. We do.

SOCRATES. A point we've examined over not days, weeks, or years, but decades.

PLATO. True.

SOCRATES. Concluding that even when a person is wronged, which most say justifies wrongdoing in return, we say wrongdoing is wrongdoing, and must in all cases be avoided.

PLATO. We do.

SOCRATES. And the same is true with injury. We must not injure another, even if we've been injured.

PLATO. Agreed.

SOCRATES. Make sure you agree Plato, because mine is not a popular opinion, one that rejects retaliation. And those who disagree on this matter cannot further deliberate together, but must hold one another in persisting contempt.

PLATO. One should not injure another even if one is injured.

SOCRATES. Now answer this: Does a good and decent person keep his agreements, or does he break them?

PLATO. It depends on the agreement, and how it was entered into.

SOCRATES. Entered into knowingly and rightly, and in every respect on terms with which one still agrees.

PLATO. Then yes.

SOCRATES. Isn't it therefore the case that should I leave here without the full consent of Athens, I am doing Athens injury?

CRITO. You'll be treating Athens justly by saving her from committing an injustice. Now please!

SOCRATES. Nicely done Crito! Very well. Plato, you be me in the act of escaping, and I will play the part of Athens and her laws.

CRITO. No! I beg the two of you!

Socrates ignores him.

SOCRATES. Socrates, by leaving here without our consent, do you not set out to destroy us?

PLATO. Destroy you? As has been stated, I set out to save you from yourself committing an injustice.

SOCRATES. You'll need first to persuade me that doing what I'm to do, which is to say meting out justice as prescribed by my laws, is somehow its opposite, which is to say unjust, and this you have not done. So I ask again: Do you not with the threat of departure against our will set out to destroy us?

PLATO. I set out to destroy nothing, but simply to save myself.

SOCRATES. But what if every citizen charged with abiding by our laws should act only for himself? Would we not have anarchy?

PLATO. We would.

SOCRATES. Then you do me injury, for surely by this we mean Athens depends on her laws, and each citizen abiding by them.

PLATO. But the ruling is unjust, and the charges leveled against me based on lies.

SOCRATES. I'm confused. Was there some clause in our agreement that allows you to determine the validity of certain of our laws and deliberations, and the invalidity of others?

PLATO. No.

SOCRATES. And wasn't it by our laws that your mother and father married? That they raised you and schooled you and fed you? Didn't we require your father to educate you into the man you became?

PLATO. All true.

SOCRATES. And haven't we given you the protection and freedom to marry, to have your own children, and raise them as you were raised? To roam our streets and engage whomever you pleased, whatever the topic?

CRITO. You condemned him for that.

SOCRATES. Who is this strange man?

PLATO. A friend.

SOCRATES. The great Socrates can no longer argue on his own?

PLATO. I never asked for his help. A moment ago he didn't even want us immersed in this discussion.

CRITO. Stop it! Both of you!

SOCRATES. *(To Crito.)* You, good sir, who would so boorishly interrupt these proceedings, say we condemned him for speaking in public.

CRITO. That's precisely what you did!

SOCRATES. I don't remember any charges other than that he

repudiated our Gods and corrupted our youth. And yet he would do violence against us by escaping? He, who just professed that wronging another, even in retaliation, is never good, he would do me this injury?

PLATO. At the very least I negate a wrong that was done to me.

SOCRATES. Leaving aside we just agreed, not once but twice, to make certain we hold this conviction, that one does not answer wrong with wrong, did we not, Socrates, in a court before a jury of five hundred and one of your peers, give you the chance within our laws to persuade us of this wrong?

CRITO. You gave him part of a day! In Sparta he would have had three, and could have called witnesses, and questioned his accusers.

SOCRATES. Was he not familiar not only with our laws, but also the manner in which we administer them?

PLATO. I was.

SOCRATES. And did we ever require you to remain here, a prisoner of our customs? Or did we, on the contrary, say that you, like any citizen of Athens, were free to leave with all your property and go to any city you pleased?

PLATO. You did.

SOCRATES. Which is why I say Socrates that you, who knew our laws, benefited from our laws, and failed on three counts against you to persuade us as to their misapplication, would do us injury by disobeying us. Moreover, should you escape, you would not only be guilty of an awful deceit, but establish yourself as one of the most heinous ever to have transgressed against us.

CRITO. Now the most heinous?!

SOCRATES. He questions Athens, it is true. Some even claim that in so doing he has intended her harm. But I ask you truly: Who has embraced Athens more than he? Who loves the people of Athens more?

CRITO. Are you really going to make this claim?

SOCRATES. I know something about the man in question. *(Pointing to Plato.)* And you'll see he doesn't deny it. *(Now speaking directly to Plato.)* You rarely leave the city, even for festivals. You wake early to be on the Agora with the sun, and have roamed every street to be among our people and devote yourself to their betterment, so much do you love them. Who is more well known? What's more, when you could have chosen banishment at your trial, you rejected it, when condemning you to live abroad would have been preferable to the jury. You also proposed a fine, but then insisted your behavior would never change, thus knowingly undermining the offer. Should you therefore, being so notorious, leave, an example of treachery to all, you would be the lowest sort of animal.

After a pause, he addresses them both.

Have we not then concluded that in service of what is good—not answering wrong with wrong, and keeping the covenant you have made with me, Athens, the city that reared, nourished, and protected you—that you, Socrates, especially you, must remain and suffer the punishment we have determined?

Neither can respond.

CRITO. What about your wife and boys?

SOCRATES. Should I do as you propose, they would either follow me into exile, where I would always be that fugitive who went against his own principles. Or they would remain here without me to be looked after by you and others, which is really no different than my death. Either way I as myself will be missing from their lives.

A brief silence.

Go and tell Xanthippe it is decided. She may come with the boys when it's light.

Crito doesn't move.

Please, Crito.

Crito leaves.

What doesn't he understand?

PLATO. I know what you think he doesn't understand. That only by seeing this through will your life have meaning. You're seventy. That Athens feared you enough to condemn you already proves your life has meaning.

SOCRATES. One thing I've learned in seventy years is that man is well suited for tyranny, but especially when that tyranny is disguised as Democracy.

PLATO. Meaning?

SOCRATES. This is no longer about me.

PLATO. I thought you weren't political.

SOCRATES. Of course I'm political.

A pause.

What I've been wrestling with here, more than anything, is my hope that my accusers be remembered for this deed, and not in a nice way.

PLATO. Who can blame you?

SOCRATES. I wish them punished. Even…harmed.

Plato smiles.

PLATO. I never heard you say it.

SOCRATES. Never heard me be human?

PLATO. You will ascend into a world far greater than this one.

SOCRATES. I'm no mystic.

PLATO. Nor am I.

SOCRATES. I can address only what's in front of me.

Plato to the Boy.

PLATO. In that way he was most like you.

BOY. I had already noticed that.

PLATO. Forgive me.

Socrates continues to Plato.

SOCRATES. Besides, it would be a crowded place, your afterlife. I'm not sure I'd be comfortable there, unless put in a room with souls of my choosing. I'd rather live on here.

PLATO. Given your determination to die, I know of only one way to ensure that.

SOCRATES. On my terms, Plato, not yours or anyone else's.

PLATO. You've been writing yourself.

SOCRATES. Poetry recounting dreams. And I've burned every

sheaf. I wish you to destroy everything you've written that bears my name.

PLATO. Even if I agreed, Xenophon has been writing about you now, and who knows how many others?

SOCRATES. They have fewer of their own ideas, making them far less dangerous. Please. If you love me.

PLATO. Because I love you. I will publish only what you have said. The dialogues precisely as they've taken place.

SOCRATES. Please... ·

PLATO. To agree to what you ask would be a lie. The most treacherous lie imaginable. I couldn't live with that, nor would you want me to.

Silence.

SOCRATES. Where we diverge make them your words, even someone else's, never mine.

PLATO. I promise.

SOCRATES. Never.

PLATO. I promise.

SOCRATES. Swear.

PLATO. I swear.

Plato and the Boy.

And there you are. A vow I have broken over and over. Put more of my words in his mouth than his own.

BOY. Why?

PLATO. Because no greater thinker will ever walk this earth.

BOY. Then why would you need to change his ideas?

PLATO. You're of course right, but I speak of the method for finding the ideas, not the ideas themselves, of which, if you've been hearing me at all, you'll understand he actually had very few.

BOY. Then...?

PLATO. If I've learned anything it's that nothing, so long as we can think it with these brains of ours, or even see it with these eyes, hear it with these ears, nothing is purely what we think it is. We get rather an approximation at best. This above all is what he taught me, in endless dialogues with countless Athenians in which stubbornly elusive truths were never discovered, no matter how hard he and his interlocutors—myself included—tried. Imagine that. An entire lifetime of pursuit, and not a single so called "truth" to show for it. Of course "taught" is a word he would never have used, and this is a concept he would never have believed.

BOY. You're not making sense.

Plato considers how to proceed.

PLATO. We've been speaking all morning about Socrates.

BOY. Yes.

PLATO. But you know just the shape of him…through my telling only, or my telling of his telling. You never met the man. As if I'd thrown a shadow of him onto that wall. My description, however elaborate, gives him no dimension, no flesh. So long as we are in our bodies, with all the corruption that entails of sight and sound and smell and their myriad combinations and distractions in our flawed, fragile, and ambitious minds, we're as far from what is true as you are from knowing Socrates. Truth is somewhere else. Something else.

BOY. Then why try to know anything at all?

PLATO. Because there is nothing more noble than the pursuit. I may disagree with much of what Socrates thought, but his manner of questioning—the sheer intuitive beauty of it, up until the moment he died, will never be matched. Never. If I offer anything to the world, as a writer or teacher—and I am a teacher—let me give that. And so yes, I broke my promise to a dying man whom I desperately loved, so that what Socrates died defending, the method and temerity to challenge all that was held dear, could live. I'd rather he speak my words in his way than I speak them in mine, if only to teach people not what to think, but how, which is far more important.

The Boy takes this in.

BOY. Were you there when he died?

PLATO. I was ill.

BOY. I know that's what you've claimed.

PLATO. You don't believe it?

BOY. I don't think there's an illness that could be experienced or even named that would have kept you away.

PLATO. I see.

A long pause.

Of course I was there.

BOY. What happened?

PLATO. What really happened?

BOY. Yes.

PLATO. We crowded the room, all of us…

Socrates surrounded by friends: Plato, Crito, Apollodorus, Simmias, Phaedo, and Antisthenes.

You know many of them by now: Crito, Simmias of Thebes, a young man named Phaedo, who like me mostly listened, another follower named Apollodorus, and Antisthenes the Cynic.

ANTISTHENES. Honestly, I would rather go mad than be happy!

CRITO. Enough, Antisthenes. We're here to listen to Socrates, not you.

BOY. What was talked about?

PLATO. The heavenly, the mundane, and in the end…what was most tragically practical.

Socrates addresses the group.

SOCRATES. Hear me out. And besides, happiness doesn't enter into it, Antisthenes, so you needn't worry. Do we admit there is such a thing as equality? And by this I mean the principle of equality itself?

PLATO. Answer.

BOY. Me?

SOCRATES. *(To the room.)* Anyone?

PLATO. It's the end of his life. Is he weeping? Bemoaning his fate? No. He's asking if there's a concept we call equality.

The Boy engages, placing himself among the others.

BOY. There is.

SOCRATES. Where do we get this idea, Plato?

BOY. From the world around us.

SOCRATES. Meaning when we see stones and logs and other objects we say are equal to one another in size and shape?

BOY. Yes.

SOCRATES. But it seems to me that on close inspection, say of two logs, we might find them similar but not precisely equal. One might be slightly longer than the other, or of greater weight and diameter.

BOY. True.

SOCRATES. So are any two things ever perfectly equal?

BOY. They never are.

SOCRATES. And yet insofar as goes the IDEA of equality, we still say it exists. Would everyone agree.

EVERYONE. Yes. We would.

SOCRATES. Which is just my problem: I don't see how we've learned equality—absolute, true equality—from physical objects, since we've just determined they'll always differ from one another in some way.

SIMMIAS. I suppose that's true.

SOCRATES. Never mind what you suppose, Simmias; what can we learn from it?

PLATO. *(To the Boy.)* Tell him.

BOY. Tell him what?

PLATO. What he's just proposed, quite casually, in the hour before his death!

SOCRATES. What can we learn from the fact that our minds summon the idea of equality without ever having experienced it?

> *The Boy addresses Socrates.*

BOY. That such notions or ideas must exist outside of us, independent of the physical world.

PLATO. Precisely.

SOCRATES. It's at least possible.

PLATO. *(To the Boy.)* But then I went further. *(To Socrates.)* Perhaps true knowledge is a kind of recollection or memory.

SOCRATES. Go on.

PLATO. If perfect concepts can't exist in the physical world, but still we grasp them, we must at one point have encountered them elsewhere.

SOCRATES. Such as where?

Plato doesn't respond.

You seem to have a notion, Plato.

Plato proceeds carefully.

PLATO. It would have to have been somehow before we were physically born.

SOCRATES. And how could that be?

PLATO. Before we came into our bodies.

SOCRATES. This I had inferred. Suddenly there's a "before we came into our bodies."

PLATO. Have we not just proven it?

SOCRATES. I assure you we have not.

PLATO. We've determined these ideas exist outside of us.

SOCRATES. Yes.

PLATO. In essence prior to our discovery of them.

SOCRATES. Perhaps.

PLATO. Does this not allude to some previous experience or state? And what is that but a kind of recollection or memory?

SOCRATES. I see.

PLATO. Which if true might argue for the extended nature of our souls. For how else could we imagine perfection as you describe it?

Plato and Socrates stare at one another in silence.

SOCRATES. Such conjecture, my dearest of all friends, I shall gladly leave to you. It is none of mine.

A long silence.

I'll have a bath now.

CRITO. A bath?

SOCRATES. It's better to drink the poison clean, so the women won't have to wash my corpse. *(To a slave.)* Is it prepared?

SLAVE. Yes.

CRITO. One of the only times you've bathed in your life, and just so you can die?

SOCRATES. If that's how you choose to see it, Crito. Bring Xanthippe and the children.

Crito goes to the cell door.

CRITO. Xanthippe.

A guard admits Xanthippe and two of Socrates's three sons: Lamprocles, in his teens, and Menexenus, a year old, held in Xanthippe's arms. They, along with Plato and Crito, follow Socrates to a shallow basin.

SOCRATES. And my middle son? Where might he be?

XANTHIPPE. Sophroniscus is ill, sir.

SOCRATES. I see.

XANTHIPPE. Ill with grief.

SOCRATES. I see.

Socrates strips and eases himself into the water.

Lamprocles.

XANTHIPPE. Say hello to your father, Lamprocles.

He doesn't.

Lamprocles.

SOCRATES. It's all right.

LAMPROCLES. I tried to comfort my brother. It's not as though your departure will make any difference. Not to us anyway.

XANTHIPPE. That's enough.

SOCRATES. You were welcome wherever I went.

LAMPROCLES. Was I?

Pause.

SOCRATES. My father taught me to work with stone. I followed him everywhere. He never asked me to come along, I just did. While he worked he never spoke, and I certainly didn't, even to ask questions, because his concentration was so severe. But after a while the rooms and open spaces where he toiled became filled

83

with his questions... very loud at first, and then hardly perceptible with his mallet and chisel, striking away with hands that fought the Persians at Marathon, looking for truth in the huge blocks of stone. I honestly don't think a word ever passed between us in perhaps thousands of hours of my apprenticeship, because in those days of course a son followed his father's trade. That's how it was done. I walked away from the future I'd been given, they said, but it's simply not true. I've spent my life applying what I learned. I just don't use stone.

Lamprocles takes this in, leaves.

XANTHIPPE. I don't think that was the answer he was looking for.

SOCRATES. It's the only one I know how to give.

XANTHIPPE. And what's your answer to me?

SOCRATES. I didn't hear a question.

XANTHIPPE. I know you didn't.

Silence.

Shall I get your back?

Socrates offers Plato the sponge.

SOCRATES. Plato will do it.

XANTHIPPE. No, I will.

SOCRATES. *(To Plato.)* You'd better hand it over or mine won't be the only corpse carried out of here.

Plato relinquishes the sponge. Xanthippe begins to clean her husband. She has begun to weep freely as she finishes. Socrates emerges, drying off and donning his clothes.

You should take the children home.

XANTHIPPE. Please...

SOCRATES. Please what?

She can't find words.

Speak what you have to say. I can't know what you don't speak.

XANTHIPPE. Even now...you don't have to go through with this...

SOCRATES. The poison is being prepared and guards are waiting outside—

XANTHIPPE. Stop it. There's enough money in this room among friends who would gladly pay it to have everyone look the other way while you're taken from Athens as we've arranged.

SOCRATES. Arranged? We meaning who? Everyone but me?

XANTHIPPE. Is being a husband and father simply not enough for you? Or being a friend to all of these men?

SOCRATES. I will not flee.

XANTHIPPE. No one is asking you to—

SOCRATES. It is precisely what you are asking!

XANTHIPPE. I'm begging you. If you care at all what I—

SOCRATES. What you what?

XANTHIPPE. What I think and feel!

SOCRATES. ARE YOU STANDING HERE WAITING TO DIE? ARE THE CHILDREN? YOUR THOUGHTS AND FEELINGS ON THIS MATTER ARE OF NO IMPORTANCE TO ME!

Silence.

XANTHIPPE. Forget the hatred and the gossip. Forget that friend after friend has fallen away as you've become more and more despised. Forget a loneliness I experience day after day you cannot possibly fathom. Forget how I've had to scrounge and beg so we don't go hungry. Forget that you've strayed from us further and further year after year. I will leave here with your boys, whom you in turn leave to the world, none of them to have the privilege you once had of being raised and protected by a father in a city, this so-called democracy that sees women as no more than vessels to bear and feed men. Where for me even to be out of doors with them is not allowed. Look at us, and then consider the boy at home stricken with despair, or the other who just left who wants nothing more than for you to know, to perceive, one little bit of him, and know this: In doing what you're about to do, you've proven what you've always claimed.

SOCRATES. And what is that?

XANTHIPPE. That you understand absolutely nothing.

He motions to Apollodorus.

SOCRATES. Take them outside.

XANTHIPPE. NOOOOOO!

Apollodorus leads the family away. Silence.

SOCRATES. You think me callous.

CRITO. No one said anything.

Silence. The guard enters.

GUARD. The sun will soon be setting.

The men absorb the meaning.

I don't write the sentences. I only carry them out as Athens orders.

SOCRATES. The citizens of Athens.

GUARD. Of everyone who's ever come here, you've been the kindest to me.

SOCRATES. From whom was I to gain better instruction regarding all of this?

GUARD. Shall I—?

SOCRATES. We'll call if you're needed.

The guard leaves.

Is it prepared?

SIMMIAS. You can eat, have some wine.

SOCRATES. I'm not going to make an idiot of myself dragging this out.

SIMMIAS. Hardly idiotic.

SOCRATES. Precisely idiotic, and I won't argue the point anymore, Simmias.

CRITO. I'll ask.

SOCRATES. Let Plato. After all, he paid for it.

PLATO. Would you rather have been strangled to death in public?

SOCRATES. This is our gift to Crito.

CRITO. How is that?

SOCRATES. By drinking the poison myself I spare Athens committing the injustice.

CRITO. I see.

SOCRATES. I am grateful to be here with you all.

Plato moves to where a poisoner grinds hemlock in a bowl.

POISONER. Almost.

PLATO. The opium will help?

POISONER. He instructed me against the opium.

PLATO. And I am instructing you otherwise.

POISONER. He requested the highest concentration as well. Regardless, this won't by any means be painless.

PLATO. Please do as I ask.

Plato back with the group.

It'll be another moment.

SOCRATES. See there Simmias, you shall have your wish.

APOLLODORUS. None of us wishes this.

SOCRATES. What did that poet say? We are all condemned by nature the day we are born.

The poisoner appears with the cup.

And by the substance of nature shall I die. *(To the poisoner.)* Tell me what to do.

The poisoner hands over the cup.

POISONER. It's simple really. Drink all of it, and then walk the room so it circulates. When your legs feel heavy, lie down and the poison will finish its work.

SOCRATES. May I offer some to the Gods as a libation?

The poisoner can't tell if this is a joke.

Surely it wouldn't harm them.

POISONER. I've measured the proper dose and no more. I'm afraid if all of it doesn't go to you...

SOCRATES. Then a prayer: that my journey be a prosperous one, for me, for those in this world, and those in dear Plato's next.

He drinks it all.

POISONER. Now begin to walk.

Men begin to weep. Socrates walks as instructed.

SOCRATES. Please. This is why I sent my wife away. Let me die without all this weeping.

Only Plato remains stolid.

Look at Plato. If you have to weep, save it for later. You should all envy me. For one, I have been spared old age, which would have been intolerable. Even more so for all of you having to watch me endure it. I die without regret or shame, and wish only the same sort of end for you all.

PHAEDO. We don't weep for you, Socrates, but for ourselves losing such a friend.

SOCRATES. And I ask that you rejoice in having had me as a friend, for this is how I feel toward each of you. I rejoice. Simply think of all we have shared...

He slows and stumbles slightly.

Quick work. *(To the poisoner.)* Quite the concoction.

The poisoner guides Socrates to the bed, where others help him to lie down.

POISONER. Ease away, all of you. Ease back. Give him room to take breath. Give him room.

Everyone but Crito does.

You too sir. Please.

Crito complies. A pause as Socrates breathes in deeply, repeatedly.

That's it. Deep breaths. Allow the poison to circulate.

After a few more breaths, the poisoner gently pinches a toe.

Can you feel this?

SOCRATES. I can't.

The poisoner reaches higher to the knee.

POISONER. This?

SOCRATES. No.

Up near the groin.

POISONER. Here?

SOCRATES. Barely.

Socrates shivers.

POISONER. You're colder?

SOCRATES. Yes.

Socrates shivers violently.

POISONER. And becoming numb here now?

SOCRATES. Yes.

POISONER. It has reached your heart and spreads from there.

SOCRATES. Mmmmm.

Socrates covers his face, the chill, the numbness and the pain, where he can feel it, beginning to overwhelm him. He uncovers, mustering a waning ability to speak.

Crito…

CRITO. Yes?

SOCRATES. We should offer a cock to Asclepius. Make sure and do this. Don't forget.

CRITO. Of course. Is there anything else?

Socrates writhes, turning away to retch violently and repeatedly, quickly giving way to a succession of terrific spasms. They are ugly and intense. He cries out uncontrollably.

Is there nothing we can do?

POSIONER. Nothing but let the poison do its work.

PLATO. I told you to mix in opium!

POISONER. You think I didn't?! This is what happens. The body fights for itself.

The men avert their eyes, all but Plato, as Socrates shakes violently, shuddering and exclaiming in pain for a long period, until he finally expires. Silence. Finally, now, Plato weeps.

PLATO. We sat all night with his body.

Dawn. The corpse is carried out and the men exit one by one.

Not until well past dawn did any of us go home, abroad into an Athens changed forever, with no turning back from what we'd done. Yes. We. Every Athenian.

The Boy looks at Plato on the empty stage.

BOY. Who was Asclepius?

PLATO. Who IS Asclepius. Not a person, but a God. Discovered by the priests in Socrates' life.

BOY. How do you discover a God?

PLATO. In spite of myself, I really think I am going to grow to like you. I have often wondered myself. Asclepius is the son of Apollo. Apollo who gives us light and reason.

BOY. Did Crito take him the rooster as Socrates asked?

> *Crito appears, holding a rooster in a cage.*

PLATO. We went together. It took days to reach the temple. In Epidaurus to the west and across the gulf.

> *Asclepius stands in marble, his hand holding a staff entwined with a serpent.*

> *Plato joins Crito. They place the cage at the base of the altar.*

BOY. But why Asclepius?

PLATO. He is the God of healing. Does it make sense to you now?

BOY. And then?

PLATO. Crito went home to see to his sons, attend to his farms, and of course help Xanthippe settle affairs, such as they were.

> *Crito leaves.*

I remained until sunset. There came many supplicants to the young God, for it was said he'd cured Athens of the plague years before.

> *Supplicants appear one by one and place offerings...live animals in cages.*

Even some members of the jury, I couldn't help but notice. I hid myself from view, wanting to think they were asking forgiveness, but suspecting it wasn't true.

> *Only the animals remain at the statue's base.*

The creatures huddled there, caged and oblivious beneath a marble God. It struck me as so gorgeously silly. And futile. And right. All of it. There we were.

> *He comes center.*

I looked out over the gulf toward home and considered a life without him. Was I now unburdened, free of his rough and tender grasp, or more tied to him than ever? I can say to you that not a day passes without his hand at my elbow, his patiently urgent voice in my ear. Did he have to die? I think so. He was what we amounted to at a moment in time, however exquisitely deluded, self-defeating, and impossible it made us and him. He exposed us to our lies, and we killed him for it.

Pause.

And the lies continue, grow more and more elaborate, pernicious, irreversible. We simply cannot help ourselves.

Silence. Plato collects himself.

But now... What do you have for me there?

BOY. It's only a beginning.

PLATO. It's late, but read me what you've brought.

After a pause, the Boy does.

BOY. Everything we do... every action... all we attempt... is thought to be aimed at some good.

PLATO. Let us only hope.

Pause.

But now... some questions...

Lights fade.

End of Play

PROPERTY LIST

(Use this space to create props lists for your production)

SOUND EFFECTS

(Use this space to create sound effects lists for your production)

Dear reader,

Thank you for supporting playwrights by purchasing this acting edition! You may not know that Dramatists Play Service was founded, in 1936, by the Dramatists Guild and a number of prominent play agents to protect the rights and interests of playwrights. To this day, we are still a small company committed to our partnership with the Guild, and by proxy all playwrights, established and aspiring, working in the English language.

Because of our status as a small, independent publisher, we respectfully reiterate that this text may not be distributed or copied in any way, or uploaded to any file-sharing sites, including ones you might think are private. Photocopying or electronically distributing books means both DPS and the playwright are not paid for the work, and that ultimately hurts playwrights everywhere, as our profits are shared with the Guild.

We also hope you want to perform this play! Plays are wonderful to read, but even better when seen. If you are interested in performing or producing the play, please be aware that performance rights must be obtained through Dramatists Play Service. This is true for *any* public performance, even if no one is getting paid or admission is not being charged. Again, playwrights often make their sole living from performance royalties, so performing plays without paying the royalty is ultimately a loss for a real writer.

This acting edition is the **only approved text for performance**. There may be other editions of the play available for sale from other publishers, but DPS has worked closely with the playwright to ensure this published text reflects their desired text of all future productions. If you have purchased a revised edition (sometimes referred to as other types of editions, like "Broadway Edition," or "[Year] Edition"), that is the only edition you may use for performance, unless explicitly stated in writing by Dramatists Play Service.

Finally, this script cannot be changed without written permission from Dramatists Play Service. If a production intends to change the script in any way—including casting against the writer's intentions for characters, removing or changing "bad" words, or making other cuts however small—without permission, they are breaking the law. And, perhaps more importantly, changing an artist's work. Please don't do that!

We are thrilled that this play has made it into your hands. We hope you love it as much as we do, and thank you for helping us keep the American theater alive and vital.

Note on Songs/Recordings, Images, or Other Production Design Elements

Be advised that Dramatists Play Service, Inc., neither holds the rights to nor grants permission to use any songs, recordings, images, or other design elements mentioned in the play. It is the responsibility of the producing theater/organization to obtain permission of the copyright owner(s) for any such use. Additional royalty fees may apply for the right to use copyrighted materials.

For any songs/recordings, images, or other design elements mentioned in the play, works in the public domain may be substituted. It is the producing theater/organization's responsibility to ensure the substituted work is indeed in the public domain. Dramatists Play Service, Inc., cannot advise as to whether or not a song/arrangement/recording, image, or other design element is in the public domain.